D1213872

SWEET CHARITY

SWEET CHARITY

Book by
Neil Simon

Music by
Cy Coleman

Words by
Dorothy Fields

RANDOM HOUSE   NEW YORK

7002439

FOR *Gwen Verdon*

SWEET CHARITY *was first presented on January 29, 1966, by Fryer, Carr and Harris at the Palace Theatre in New York City with the following cast:*

(In order of appearance)

CHARITY	Gwen Verdon
DARK GLASSES	Michael Davis
BYSTANDER	John Stratton
MARRIED COUPLE	Bud Vest, Elaine Cancilla
WOMAN WITH HAT	Ruth Buzzi
ICE CREAM VENDOR	Gene Foote
FOOTBALL PLAYER	John Sharpe
BALLPLAYERS	Harold Pierson, Eddie Gasper
CAREER GIRL	Barbara Sharma
SPANISH YOUNG MAN	Darrell Notara
FIRST COP	John Wheeler
SECOND COP	David Gold
HELENE	Thelma Oliver
NICKIE	Helen Gallagher
CARMEN	Carmen Morales
HERMAN	John Wheeler
DOORMAN	I. W. Klein
URSALA	Sharon Ritchie
VITTORIO VIDAL	James Luisi
WAITER	John Stratton
MANFRED	Bud Vest
RECEPTIONIST	Ruth Buzzi
OLD MAID	Elaine Cancilla
OSCAR	John McMartin
DADDY JOHANN SEBASTIAN BRUBECK	Arnold Soboloff
BROTHER HAROLD	Harold Pierson
BROTHER EDDIE	Eddie Gasper
POLICEMAN	Harold Pierson
ROSIE	Barbara Sharma
BARNEY	David Gold

| MIKE | Michael Davis |
| GOOD FAIRY | Ruth Buzzi |

THE SINGERS AND DANCERS OF TIMES SQUARE: I. W. Klein, Mary Louise, Alice Evans, Betsy Dickerson, Kathryn Doby, Suzanne Charny, Elaine Cancilla, Carmen Morales, Christine Stewart, Charlene Ryan, David Gold, Gene Foote, Harold Pierson, Bud Vest, Darrell Notara, John Sharpe, Eddie Gasper, Michael Davis, Patrick Heim.

Book by Neil Simon

Music by Cy Coleman

Lyrics by Dorothy Fields

Conceived, staged and choreographed by Bob Fosse

Scenery and lighting by Robert Randolph

Musical direction and dance music arranged by Fred Werner

Costumes designed by Irene Sharaff

Orchestrations by Ralph Burns

Production manager: Robert Linden

Associate producer: John Bowab

Based on an original screenplay by Federico Fellini, Tullio Pinelli and Ennio Flaiano

Synopsis of Scenes

Act One

SCENE 1: The park.

SCENE 2: The Hostess Room of the Fan-Dango Ball-room.

SCENE 3: The Fan-Dango Ballroom.

SCENE 4: The street outside the Pompeii Club.

SCENE 5: The interior of the Pompeii Club.

SCENE 6: Vittorio Vidal's apartment.

SCENE 7: The Hostess Room of the Fan-Dango Ball-room.

SCENE 8: The Ninety-second Street "Y."

Act Two

SCENE 1: The Ninety-second Street "Y."

SCENE 2: The Rhythm of Life Church.

SCENE 3: On a New York street, going cross-town.

SCENE 4: Charity's apartment.

SCENE 5: Coney Island.

SCENE 6: The Fan-Dango Ballroom.

SCENE 7: Times Square.

SCENE 8: Barney's Chile Hacienda.

SCENE 9: The Fan-Dango Ballroom.

SCENE 10: The park.

MUSICAL NUMBERS

ACT ONE

You Should See Yourself	Charity
The Rescue	The Passers-by
Big Spender	Nickie, Helene and the Fan-Dango Girls
Charity's Soliloquy	Charity
Rich Man's Frug	The Patrons
If My Friends Could See Me Now	Charity
Too Many Tomorrows	Vittorio Vidal
There's Gotta Be Something Better than This	Charity, Nickie and Helene

ACT TWO

I'm the Bravest Individual	Charity and Oscar
Rhythm of Life	Daddy Brubeck, Brother Harold, Brother Eddie and Worshippers
Baby, Dream Your Dream	Nickie and Helene
Sweet Charity	Oscar
Where Am I Going?	Charity
I'm a Brass Band	Charity and her Brass Band
I Love to Cry at Weddings	Herman, Nickie and Helene, Girls and Patrons

Act One

The stage is in darkness. There is music, "Charity's Theme." A light picks up a girl, CHARITY. *She carries a shoulder bag. High on her left arm is a small heart-shaped tattoo. Across the heart, a man's name is tattooed. She begins to walk aimlessly about the stage. This soon develops into a dance. As she is dancing, a sign descends. (Periodically throughout the play, signs will appear. Some will fly, some will be pushed out from the portals and some will be carried across the stage, perhaps done in fluorescent paint, to be seen in the dark.)*

A light hits this first sign. It reads: "THE ADVENTURES OF CHARITY." A second sign appears. It reads: "THE STORY OF A . . ." A third sign says: "GIRL WHO WANTED TO BE . . ."

There is a momentary pause. Then a fourth sign appears. It reads: "LOVED."

This fourth sign is decorated like a valentine. All four signs disappear. The dance ends.

The lights come up to reveal a park containing several groupings of trees and perhaps a bench or two. The audience should know that the orchestra pit is the lake.

CHARITY *begins to look around for someone. A young man wearing dark glasses enters. He too seems to be looking for someone. He has a great deal of black wavy hair which he combs constantly. Suddenly they both turn and see each other. He is about to speak when* CHARITY *holds up her hand.*

CHARITY Charlie, don't—don't say a word. Because I know exactly what you're gonna say. I've been thinking about it all day. You're gonna start off with (*She primps*

3

her hair, then sniffs) . . . "Mmm, that heavenly odor. Is that perfume or is that you?" And then you're gonna look in my eyes and say (*She looks in his eyes, tiger-like*), "You drive me crazy, did you know that? Did you know you drive me crazy?" And then—you're gonna take my hand and hold it in yours (*She takes his hand in hers*) . . . and then—and this is the best part—then you're gonna say, "Honey, you are the sweetest, the softest, the prettiest girl in this whole cockeyed crazy wide wonderful world." (*She sighs*) Oh, brother, you sure know how to talk to a girl. (*She sings*)

Man! Man, oh, man!
Tst—tst—tst—
You should see yourself . . . You're a sight.
You're a hundred watt e-lec-a-tric light.
You're a block-buster, Buster; you got class.
And when *you* make a pass, man, it's a pass!
Man! Jack, you're mad! Mmmmmmmmmmmm!
How those corny jokes turn me on!
And I laugh till I'm ga-ga-ga-ga-gone!
When you switch to a se-duc-a-tive mood
I'm not stuck on you, lover, I am glued!
In that college-type rah-rah-dee-dah tweed
Do I wilt? Boy, are you built!
You're so strong, you got muscles you don't need!
Yes . . . Yes, indeed!
Wild! Dad, you're wild! Grrrrrrrrrrrr!
You should see yourself in my eyes!
You're a blue ribbon Pul-it-itzer prize!
   (*Speaks*)

You know what I did today? I looked at furniture. Bedroom sets, kitchen sets, bedroom sets, living room sets, bedroom sets. (*They walk toward the orchestra pit*) And I've got the money for the down payment right here. My dowry. (*She sings*)

Dreams . . . I had not!

Dreams . . . now I got!

You're Old Glory, man; yes, you are!

In my flag, you're the fi-fifty-first star!

You should see yourself . . . and inspect yourself,

Get a mirror, man, and reflect yourself.

You should see yourself as I see you now!

(*They stop at the "lake"*)

Charlie, doesn't the lake look beautiful? (*She takes off a shoe and "dips" her toes into the "water"*) Oooh, it feels nice . . . Hey, Charlie, let's throw something in the lake for luck. (DARK GLASSES *quickly looks around, then in one cat-like movement, he grabs* CHARITY's *shoulder bag and shoves her into the "lake." A sign appears. It reads: "SPLASH!" It disappears.* DARK GLASSES *runs off.* CHARITY's *voice comes from the pit*) Help! Help!

(*A sign appears. It reads: "THE RESCUE." It disappears. Music begins.*

FIRST PASSER-BY *enters. He hears the calls. He slowly walks to the edge of the stage and looks down. He shakes his head and says, "Tsk. Tsk." He exits.*

A MARRIED COUPLE *strolls by. The cries for help continue*)

MARRIED WOMAN (*Pointing*)   Look, Walter, there's a girl in there drowning.

MARRIED MAN (*Looks and turns away*)   Don't look, dear.

MARRIED WOMAN   But Walter—

MARRIED MAN   Don't look, I tell you. Don't get involved. It's none of our business.

(*They look away. The* FOOTBALL PLAYER *enters and sees* CHARITY *in the water*)

FOOTBALL PLAYER (*Calling to someone*)   Hey, there's a girl in there. I think she's drowning.

(A WOMAN WITH A HAT *rushes in and stands next to the* FOOTBALL PLAYER. *She peers into the pit*)

WOMAN WITH HAT   Yes, it certainly looks like she's drowning.
(An ICE CREAM VENDOR *rushes in*)

ICE CREAM VENDOR   What's going on?

WOMAN WITH HAT (*Points*)   That attractive young girl is drowning.

TALL MAN (*Entering*)   What did she say?
(A *crowd slowly begins to gather. They all ad lib about* CHARITY's *drowning. Some are on bikes, some with baseball bats, one with a kite, another with a balloon*)

FOOTBALL PLAYER   See! She's gone down two, three times already.

ICE CREAM VENDOR   Ice cream! Get your ice cream!

TALL MAN   Over here!

FOOTBALL PLAYER   Jeez, I don't think she can even swim.

SECOND WOMAN   Sure doesn't look like it.

WOMAN WITH HAT (*Cupping her hands, yells down to* CHARITY)   You should've taken swimming lessons. Now it's too late.

BASEBALL PLAYER (*To another*)   Hey, I'll get my kid brother. He's never seen a drowning.

ICE CREAM VENDOR   Soda! Ice cold soda!

GIRL   Here.
(A MAN WITH A DOG *enters*)

MAN WITH DOG   What's going on? What's happened?

MARRIED MAN   There's a girl in the lake. Looks like she's drowning.

MAN WITH DOG   Drowning? There's a girl drowning and you all just stand around? My God, why doesn't somebody do something?

WOMAN WITH HAT   Why don't you?

MAN WITH DOG (*Indignant*)   I can't. I'm walking my dog.

SPANISH YOUNG MAN   She's floating over here. I get her. Here, Señorita, here.
   (*He gets down on his knees*)

MARRIED MAN   What's happening now?

SECOND WOMAN   The Spanish man is going to help her.

WOMAN WITH HAT (*Disgusted*)   I certainly wouldn't let one of *them* help *me*.

SPANISH YOUNG MAN (*Leans way over*)   My ankles. Somebody hold my ankles.

ICE CREAM VENDOR   Peanuts! Hot roasted peanuts!

SPANISH YOUNG MAN   Over here, Señorita.
   (*Two* HUSKY YOUNG MEN *grab his ankles*)

SECOND WOMAN   I wish they'd hurry. I have a three o'clock dentist appointment.

FOOTBALL PLAYER   He's got her! He's got her!
   (CHARITY's *hands reach for the* SPANISH YOUNG MAN's)

AD LIBS   "Look, he's got her," etc.

BASEBALL PLAYER   Atta boy, baby.
   (*He slaps the* SPANISH YOUNG MAN *very hard on the back, causing him to drop* CHARITY. *There is another splash*)

7

FOOTBALL PLAYER Aw, butterfingers!

BASEBALL PLAYER Oh, oh. She's gone under.

ICE CREAM VENDOR Last call for ice cream!

FOOTBALL PLAYER There she is. He's got her again.
> (*And with a big heave, the* SPANISH YOUNG MAN *hauls* CHARITY *out of the water. All ad lib their encouragement. She is soaking wet and in a state of semi-consciousness. They place her on the floor and the crowd gathers around her*)

ALL We did it.
> (*There is a moment of contemplative silence*)

SECOND WOMAN She looks dead. Does she look dead to you?

MARRIED MAN I don't know. I never saw her before.

FOOTBALL PLAYER What'll we do?

MARRIED MAN Artificial respiration.

AD LIBS "Very good." "Good idea," etc.
> (*A* DIRTY OLD MAN, *who looks like a dirty old man, steps forward. He has a lecherous smile*)

DIRTY OLD MAN No, no. Mouth to mouth—mouth to mouth resuscitation.
> (*He starts to move toward* CHARITY *and a* THIRD WOMAN *shoves him back*)

MARRIED WOMAN Get away from her, you dirty old man.

DIRTY OLD MAN I just wanted to give her mouth to mouth—

MARRIED WOMAN I know what you wanted to give her. Get outa here!

8

BASEBALL PLAYER   Upside down. We gotta get the water out.

FOOTBALL PLAYER   Yeah, c'mon. Upside down.
(*Three or four men pick* CHARITY *up and hold her by the legs, upside down. Ad libs. They shake her.* CHARITY *begins to come out of it*)

WOMAN WITH HAT   Look, she's beginning to open her eyes. (*Ad libs*) Quiet, everybody; quiet.
(CHARITY, *still upside down, opens her eyes. She looks around*)

CHARITY   . . . Oh, my God, I'm in Australia!

MARRIED WOMAN   She's all right.
(*Ad libs*)

CHARITY   Put me down! Put me down! Will you put me down! (*They turn* CHARITY *over and put her down as she starts swinging at all the men*) What do you think you're doing, you—you bunch of degenerates.

WOMAN WITH HAT   I beg your pardon.

CHARITY   Is this how you get your kicks, lady?

FOOTBALL PLAYER   Take it easy. You was drowning.

BASEBALL PLAYER   Wow, what a stupid broad.

FOOTBALL PLAYER   Maybe she was trying to knock herself off.

BASEBALL PLAYER   Sure. Over some guy.

CHARITY (*Indignant*)   Ha. That's a laugh. I've got everything to live for. I'm a normal, desirable and much sought after young woman who can have any man she

9

wants at the snap of her fingers. (*She snaps her fingers twice, but there's no sound*) They're a little wet.
(*They all laugh*)

FOOTBALL PLAYER   I think *you're* a little wet, lady.

CHARITY   How would you like a soggy fist right in your big mouth?
(*She swings at him. There is about to be a fight when* TWO POLICEMEN *enter the crowd*)

FIRST COP   All right; all right, break it up. Let's break it up, heh? What's going on here?

SECOND COP   Let's break it up.
(*All the people in the crowd now offer up their version of how the rescue took place. It is a garble.* CHARITY *is now stretched out on the ground*)

BASEBALL PLAYER   Ah, this stupid broad was drowning, and I . . .
(CHARITY *swings at him again*)

FIRST COP   Hey, take it easy, lady.

CHARITY (*To* COP)   Where were you when I needed you?

FIRST COP   Let's move along, heh? The excitement's all over.

TALL MAN   Don't you push me. I'm a taxpayer.
(*The* SECOND COP *begins to shoo away the people, who leave reluctantly.* CHARITY *discovers she only has one shoe on and begins to look for the other one*)

FIRST COP (*To* CHARITY)   All right, lady?

CHARITY (*Looking for her shoe*)   I'm fine. Fine. I feel fine. I'm very fine. Put it down in your little book. "Crazy drowned lady feels fine."

SECOND COP   You wanna tell us what happened?

CHARITY   I lost my shoe, that's what happened.

SECOND COP (*To the* FIRST COP)   Hey, Monte, look for her shoe.

CHARITY   Yeah, look for it, Monte.

FIRST COP   What did it look like?

CHARITY (*Indicating the other shoe*)   Like this one! (*Mimicking*) What'd it look like?
  (*The* FIRST COP *looks for the shoe*)

SECOND COP (*Writing in his book*)   What's your name, Miss?

CHARITY (*Looking for her shoe*)   Charity. Charity Hope Valentine.

FIRST COP (*Looks up and snickers*)   Charity Hope Valentine?

CHARITY   I wouldn't snicker at other people's names, Monte!

SECOND COP   Address?

CHARITY   615 West Ninety-fourth Street.

SECOND COP   Occupation?

CHARITY   . . . I'm a Social Consultant.

SECOND COP   Where?

CHARITY   The Fan-Dango Ballroom.

SECOND COP (*Looks at her, then writes in his book*)   Dance hall hostess.

FIRST COP   You mean you work in one of them tango palaces?

CHARITY It's temporary.

SECOND COP Length of employment?

CHARITY Eight years. Oh, there's my shoe. In the water. Monte, would you be a sweet cop and—

FIRST COP (*Reluctantly*) Yeah, yeah.
        (*He leans down into the "lake"*)

CHARITY He's a sweet cop.
        (MONTE *has the shoe out. He hands it to her*)

SECOND COP All right, I'd like to know what you were doing in the water.

CHARITY Actually, very little. You see, my fiancé, Charlie—that's his name on my tattoo—well, he's not really my fiancé. We're engaged to be wed the minute his own marriage breaks up, which, if you ask me, looks like it's on the rocks right now. Anyway . . . Thank you, Monte. (*Her shoe is on and she stands*) Anyway . . . Ich, they squish. Anyway—where was I?

SECOND COP (*Looks at his book*) Anyway—
        (*A sign appears. It reads: "FAN-DANGO BALL-ROOM . . . THAT NIGHT"*)

CHARITY . . . Anyway, we had an appointment to meet in the park because naturally we can't meet at his place—his wife is very peculiar. Well, I took my shoe off and . . . put my foot in the water . . .

End of scene

The Hostess Room of the Fan-Dango Ballroom. It is a combination locker room, dressing room and lounge. CHARITY *is now in front of her locker changing. Eight or nine dance hostesses are also changing and listening to* CHARITY'S *sad story.*

CHARITY (*Continuing*) . . . my feet are always hot, you know . . . and I slipped.

GIRLS   Yeah. Sure.

CHARITY   He grabbed for me but all he got was my handbag and I fell in . . .

GIRLS   Oh, sure.

CHARITY   He started to come in after me but he didn't because of his bad back, which he received in the army —although he's very athletic, has a wonderful build, plays handball and the horses. Anyway, he ran off to get help—
   (*She is now out of her dress and into a robe. She takes a bath towel out of the locker. On the inside door of the locker there is a large, life-size picture of* DARK GLASSES)

HELENE   Honey, didn't you leave a tiny little detail out of that story?

CHARITY   Like what?

HELENE   Like there ain't one word of truth in it.
   (NICKIE *enters*)

NICKIE   Hello, men.

CARMEN Hey, Nickie, did you hear about Charity and her new boy friend?

NICKIE Oh! They're gonna be married! (*Embraces* CHARITY) Honey, all the luck in the world!

CARMEN He stole her money and pushed her in the lake.

NICKIE He wasn't for you!
  (HERMAN, *the manager, sticks his head in*)

HERMAN Awright, ladies, Prince Philip just walked in, so stick your gum behind your ears and drag it out on the floor.
  (*He exits*)

CHARITY (*Still trying*) I bet Charlie is out there right this minute. With a perfectly logical explanation. You'll see.

NICKIE Aw, baby, look—you know that I, Nickie Pignatelli, does not like to say harsh or cruel things. Despite the fact that I may have spent a few quiet years in an upstate government hotel, I am still warm, kindhearted, and basically sincere. (*To the others*) True?

HELENE True.

CARMEN True.

NICKIE True. So as a friend, someone who cares and loves you, I feel I owe ya this—you're a stupid broad! Your big problem is you run your heart like a hotel— you got guys checkin' in and out all the time.

CHARITY But this time it's different. I did slip. He wouldn't push me. He loves me. Every time I say to him, "I love you," he always says, "Ditto." "Ditto;" that's just the way he says it. Does that sound like a man who would push a girl in the lake for two hundred bucks?

NICKIE Right.

HELENE Ditto.

CARMEN Forget him, honey. We got a living to make (*They start to exit*) . . . if you call this a living.

CHARITY (*Sits at the dressing table and sings*)
　　You should see yourself, like tonight
　　You're a hundred watt e-lec-a-tric light
　　You're a block-buster. Buster, you got class
　　And when you make a pass . . . man,
　　It's a . . .
　　　(*She goes off. The Hostess Room disappears*)

End of scene

The Fan-Dango Ballroom. NICKIE, HELENE, SISSIE *and the girls are on stage.*

FIRST GIRL   Hey, mister, can I talk to you for a minute? What's the harm in a little talk?

SECOND GIRL   Hey, good-looking, I like your hair.

THIRD GIRL   Hey, mister, gotta cigarette for me?

FOURTH GIRL   Hey, mister, you speak French? Come here, I wanna talk to you.

FIFTH GIRL   Hey, fella, ya wanna dance? A little dance won't hurt ya.

SIXTH GIRL   What's the harm in talking? It can't hurt ya, can it?

SEVENTH GIRL   He's so tall . . . Must be six foot four . . .

EIGHTH GIRL   Let's have some fun.

HELENE   Psst . . .
    (NICKIE *whistles*)

ALL (*They sing*)
    The minute you walked in the joint
    I could see you were a man of distinction,
    A real big spender,
    Good looking, so refined.
    Say, wouldn't you like to know what's going on in
        my mind?
    So let me get right to the point.
    I don't pop my cork for ev'ry guy I see.
    Hey! Big spender,
    Spend a little time with me . . . me . . .

Do you wanna have . . . fun?
How about a few . . . laughs?
I can show you a good time.
Do you wanna have fun . . . fun . . .
   (They split up)
Fun . . . fun . . . fun . . . fun . . .
   (Singing together)
How about a few . . . laughs . . . laughs . . .
Fun . . . laughs . . . fun . . . laughs . . . fun . . .
    laughs . . . fun . . . laughs . . .
I can . . . show you a . . . good time . . .

Fun . . . laughs . . . good time . . .
Hey! Big spender,
Spend a little time with me.

FIRST GIRL What do you say to a . . .

SECOND GIRL How's about a . . .

ALL Laugh.

THIRD GIRL I could give you some . . .

FOURTH GIRL Are you ready for some . . .

ALL Fun.

FIFTH GIRL How would you like a . . .

SIXTH GIRL Let me show you a . . .

ALL Good time. *(They sing)*
Hey! Big spender!
Hey! Big spender!
The minute you walked in the joint
I could see you were a man of distinction,
A real big spender,
Good looking, so refined.

Say, wouldn't you like to know what's going on in
   my mind?
So let me get right to the point.
I don't pop my cork for ev'ry guy I see.
Hey! Big spender!
Hey! Big spender!
Hey! Big spender,
Spend a little time with me.
Fun, laughs, good time . . .
Fun, laughs, good time . . .
Fun, laughs, good time . . .

NICKIE   How 'bout it, palsy?

ALL   Yeah.
   (*A few of the girls walk off to the booths with men.*
   CHARITY *enters. She is looking for* DARK GLASSES)

CHARITY   Anyone ask for me?

NICKIE (*To* CHARITY)   Baby, Jack the Pusher ain't coming tonight.

CHARITY (*Still looking*)   He'll come. Like he's come every
night for the last two months, with a gardenia in his
lapel and a cigarette dangling from his lips . . .

HELENE   And a pound and a half of Vaseline in his hair.

NICKIE   I bet that's why he never wore a hat. It kept sliding off his head.

CHARITY   He *will* be here tonight. I know it. He will. He
will. He will.

NICKIE   He won't.

CHARITY   I know he won't. (*In tears*) Oh, Nickie, I'm the
biggest pushover that ever lived.

HERMAN (*From the ticket booth*) Hey, c'mon!
  (*A customer enters and selects a girl*)

CARMEN If he stole your purse, why don't you call the cops? They could still pick him up.

HELENE Sugar, you know how many guys there are running around this city with pocketbooks?

CHARITY Nickie!

NICKIE Aw, baby!
  (*She embraces her*)

CHARITY Nickie, why did he do it; why? I bought him everything he ever wanted. I even got him a midnight-blue mohair seventy-nine-dollar Italian suit that he could have bought for forty-five at Howard's. But that louse wouldn't wear a Howard's suit—

NICKIE Go ahead, honey; get it out of your system.

CHARITY The things I used to do for him. Getting up in the middle of the night to get him a provolone sandwich and a bottle of Yoo-Hoo chocolate milk.

NICKIE Men—they got no feelings.

CHARITY (*To the picture of* DARK GLASSES) Well, I've had it up to here, mister. You can slip and slide your greasy head on some other girl's shoulder.

NICKIE You tell him, baby.

CHARITY I hope your tight Italian pants choke you to death.

HELENE *Ole!*

HELENE The kid's gonna be all right.

NICKIE Yeah.

CHARITY   It won't happen to me again. How did it all
   start anyway? (*She sings*)
   Can I remember
   How this song and dance began?
   Yes, I can . . . Damned right I can.
   It began, well, anyway, ya see,
   There was this man . . .
   Who stopped and asked me if I knew
   Which way was Lexington Avenue.
   He said: "I'm going to Bloomingdale's."
   I said: "I'm going to Bloomingdale's!"
   So . . . we hoofed it over to Bloomingdale's!
      (*Speaking*)
He wanted to buy some jockey shorts! (*Singing*)
   Then he said: "Miss, would you like a cup
   O' tea or maybe some Seven-Up?"
      (*She nods and smiles; a pause*)
   I left the tip! Picked up the tab
   For the jockey shorts
   And a taxi-cab!
      (*Speaking*)
He dropped me off and I burned! Let that be a lesson
to you. Lower the boom, girl! Lower the boom! (*Sing-
ing*)
   But what can you do when he knocks on your door
   'Cause they locked him out of his furnished room!
      (*Speaking*)
So he moves in! (CHARITY *moves into the Ballroom sec-
tion. The music changes to a Bossa Nova. She smiles at
a customer, takes his tickets and dances with him. Her
soliloquy continues*) He moves in with the jockey shorts
in a paper bag! Nothing else! (*Singing*)
   He needs toothpaste
   And a tooth brush and pajama tops.

He needs razor blades, a razor and a comb! Several!
He needs sistering and brothering
And fathering and mothering.
He needs a hat
To hang up in my flat
And call it home!

In no time at all
I find we're very much in love
And I'm blushing like a sentimental slob!
And he's kissing me
And hugging me
And all the time he's bugging me
To go out and try to find myself
A better-paying job!

Comes July, it's ninety-eight degrees,
He wants a coat!
Wants a fur-lined coat. Fur collar! Cuffs! The works
      (plus tax)!
While I really didn't begrudge it,
When I figured out my budget,
For that coat I had to dance
With something like eleven hundred jerks!
      (*Speaking*)
All right, Marvin—let's not get overheated.

MARVIN   Aw—I'm nuts about you, Charity. What do you
say we spend the weekend together in Atlantic City?
I'm crazy for you.

CHARITY   Sure. The next thing you know I believe him
—and then I'm paying for the train tickets, the hotel bill,
the salt-water taffy, three Turkish baths and a massage.
(*Singing*)

Pocket money! Poker money! Smoking money!
Skating money! Bowling money! Movie money!
Haircut money! Shoe shine money!
Money for a bill from Louie's Bar.
Money for a bill from Charlie's Bar.
Money for a bill from Maxie's Bar.
But, will he ask for subway money?
No! He don't want subway money!

(*Speaking*)

'Cause it turns out the bum wants to go to Florida.
C'mon down!

MARVIN   What's your answer, Charity?

CHARITY   Here's my answer, Marvin. (*Singing*)
Now hear this!
And get this!
Oh, Susannah! Amen!
This big, fat heart
Ain't gonna be torn apart
Ever, ever, ever again! *Ole!*

(*Pushes* MARVIN *into a booth*)

My problem is I'm too giving. I'm always giving and I
never get. (*A Panhandler starts across*) Well, I'm
through giving. I already gave and *I'm not giving any
more.*

(*A* LADY *with a collection box crosses*)

LADY (*Pleadingly*)   Could you please give to the Unwed
Mothers of New York?

CHARITY   With humane pleasure.

(*She gives the* LADY *a dollar. The* LADY *starts off*)

LADY (*Tearfully*)   Thank you and bless you.

CHARITY   Er, are you an unwed mother?

LADY   No, but my mother is!
    (*She walks off*)

CHARITY (*Out front*)   Sometimes we don't know when we're well off.
    (*Three people cross quickly*)

MAN (*With box*)   Could you please give to wipe out whooping cough?

CHARITY (*Gives*)   Whooping cough? By all means.

ANOTHER LADY (*With box*)   Stamp out sex in our schools.

CHARITY (*Giving*)   I certainly want to do that.

ANOTHER MAN (*With box*)   Help put a gypsy in Congress.

CHARITY (*Giving*)   It's the least I can do.

End of scene

The street outside the Pompeii Club. A DOORMAN *stands outside by the Pompeii's canopy.*

CHARITY (*Out front*) See what I mean? Now I'm starving to death and I gave away my last nickel. (*To the* DOORMAN, *cupping her hands as if begging*) Give to a hungry dance hall hostess.

DOORMAN No soliciting, please.

CHARITY (*Making a fist*) Now just a minute, Napoleon . . .
> (*Suddenly the door of the club bursts open and a beautiful, well-groomed girl,* URSALA, *storms out. She is fuming*)

URSALA (*Throws her sable around her, angrily*) Get me a taxi right away. I'm going home.
> (*The door bursts open again and* VITTORIO VIDAL, *a mature, popular leading man in movies on both continents, rushes after her*)

VIDAL Ursala! Ursala, wait a minute. (*He crashes into* CHARITY) Excuse me, Signorina. I'm very sorry. Forgive me.

CHARITY (*Suddenly her mouth drops as she realizes who he is*) Vittorio Vidal! (*Rushes to the* DOORMAN, *pushing him*) That's Vittorio Vidal, the movie star!

VIDAL (*To* URSALA) Ursala, you've got to let me explain.

CHARITY (*Punches the* DOORMAN) Oh! It's really him. Look! Look!

VIDAL I just said "Hello" to the girl. That's all.

URSALA (*Pulls away*) Don't touch me. We're through, Vittorio. I hate you, do you hear? I hate the sight of you.

CHARITY (*To the* DOORMAN) Gee, she really knows him.

VIDAL Ursala, you can't walk out on me like this.

URSALA No? Just watch me. *Just watch me!*

CHARITY (*To the* DOORMAN) Watch! You're not watching!

VIDAL You're coming back inside. (*Aside, angrily*) How will it look for a big star like me to be alone in a night club without a girl.

URSALA That's *your* problem. (*To the* DOORMAN) Where's my taxi?

CHARITY (*Calls out*) Taxi! Taxi!

DOORMAN (*To* CHARITY) Will you get out of here!

VIDAL You're coming inside!

URSALA I'm not!

VIDAL You are!

URSALA I'm not!

VIDAL Oh, yes, you are.
    (*He pulls her*)

URSALA Oh, no, I'm not. You two-bit, "B" picture, fading Romeo. I wouldn't be caught dead seen with you. You wanna go back in there, get yourself another girl!

VIDAL But Ursala. (*All the action freezes. A sign appears. It reads: "A STROKE OF LUCK"*) Ursala! (*He knocks into* CHARITY *again*) Signorina, I'm very sorry. Forgive me.

CHARITY My pleasure.
    (*He turns and points to* CHARITY)

25

VIDAL   You. Are you busy tonight?

CHARITY (*Nudges the* DOORMAN)   He wants to know if you're busy tonight.

VIDAL (*Points*)   No. *You*. (CHARITY *looks around, then indicates herself*) Yes, you. Are you busy tonight?

CHARITY (*Gulps, then innocently*)   What time?

VIDAL   Now! Right now!

CHARITY   Right now is very good for me.

URSALA   You wouldn't dare. A girl off the streets?

VIDAL   Wouldn't I? (*To* CHARITY) Come.
         (*As he goes into the club*)

URSALA   Vittorio, you wouldn't! You wouldn't!

CHARITY (*Not viciously*)   He did. (*She takes* VIDAL'S *arm and starts to enter the club. Just as she is about to pass the bewildered* DOORMAN, *she stops and looks up at him and says proudly*) I'm with him.
         (*The rest of the stage un-freezes. The sign disappears and the street moves off*)

End of scene

The interior of the Pompeii Club, with tables and a dance floor. There are about five couples on the floor doing the "Rich Man's Frug." They continue with bits and pieces of the dance interspersed throughout the dialogue of this scene.

As VIDAL *and* CHARITY *enter, the* DANCERS *all stop dead in their tracks from the shock of seeing this great celebrity with this strange little girl.* VIDAL *looks indifferent but* CHARITY *struts as proud as a peacock.*

The astounded WAITER *shows them to their table as the others form a group and start buzzing like hens.*

FIRST DANCER Who's that with Vittorio?

SECOND DANCER What happened to Ursala?

THIRD DANCER That's not the girl he came in with.

FOURTH DANCER I've never seen her before.

FIFTH DANCER Who could she be?

SIXTH DANCER She doesn't look familiar.

SEVENTH DANCER Who is it?

EIGHTH DANCER Who is it?

NINTH DANCER Who is it?

TENTH DANCER Who is it?

ELEVENTH DANCER Who is it?

TWELFTH DANCER Who is it?

ALL Who is it?

(CHARITY, *passing by, chatting animatedly with* VIDAL, *looks up at them*)

CHARITY It's me! (*She and* VIDAL *sit as the* WAITER *hands* CHARITY *a huge menu*) Oh, isn't this gay!

WAITER Monsieur Vidal?

VIDAL A double Scotch.

WAITER (*To* CHARITY) And for Madam?

CHARITY (*She picks up the huge menu and sits*) I'll just browse for a while.
          (*She buries her head behind it*)

VIDAL (*Angrily, thinking of* URSALA) I just wish I knew what she wanted. You know she gets insane if I just look at another woman? Wouldn't you call that psychotic?

CHARITY (*Reading from the menu*) "Boy-yew de bwef oh natch-yew-rolle."

VIDAL You tell me. What do *you* think it is?

CHARITY Pot roast.

VIDAL And yet in some ways she's so vital. So exciting and full of life . . .

CHARITY Do you think we could have some rolls while we're waiting?

VIDAL (*Grabs her wrists*) Talk to me.

CHARITY (*Quickly*) Yes, Vittorio?

VIDAL You look like a normal, sensible girl.

CHARITY (*A spark of hope*) I try to dress simply.

28

VIDAL   Wouldn't you say she was vital and brimming with life?

CHARITY   That was my immediate reaction.

VIDAL   And yet she can be childish, neurotic, impossible.

CHARITY   That was my second impression.

VIDAL   Why are women like that? I've never met a man I couldn't depend on. Have you?

CHARITY   I depend on them all the time.

VIDAL   Is she worth all this? Is she?

CHARITY   Well, as you say, she *is* vital and brimming with life . . .

VIDAL   That's true. She *is* vital and brimming with life.

CHARITY   But of course, *you* know her better than I do.

VIDAL   No, no, you're right. She *is* vital and brimming with life.

CHARITY   (*To herself*) I think I just screwed myself up. (*The* WAITER *comes over with a telephone and plugs it in by their table*)

WAITER   Telephone, Monsieur Vidal.

VIDAL   Aha, it's her. Begging for forgiveness. She'll cry and plead for me to come to her apartment. What should I do? Should I be magnanimous or should I be aloof?

CHARITY   Aloof. The aloofer the better.

VIDAL   You're right. (*Into the telephone*) I'm not here. (*To* CHARITY *as he hangs up the phone*) Now I'm hungry. (*To the* WAITER) Bring us two Chateaubriand.

29

CHARITY (*To the* WAITER) May I use the phone? I'd like
to check with my telephone serv-eece!
(*She dials*)

WAITER Very good, sir. Two Chateaubriand.

CHARITY And trim the fat. (*Into the phone*) Hello,
Nickie, Miss Valentine speaking. (*She is putting on
airs*) Miss Valentine. Any messages for me? Charity,
jerk! Who called? Jerry, the Greek? (*To* VIDAL) Must
have been an overseas call. (*Back into the phone*) Oh,
well, I don't know what time I'll be home. That's en-
tirely up to Vittorio. Vittorio Vidal. Yes, the international
film star. We're sitting together at a table at the Pompeii
Club waiting for our rolls. Oh, all right. (*She hands*
VIDAL *the phone*) Would you please say hello?

VIDAL (*Into the phone*) Hello.

CHARITY (*Into the phone*) There's your hello. Now goodbye.
(*She hangs up. The music starts*)

VIDAL I seem to have done nothing but talk about my
own problems. It must be very boring.

CHARITY Well, I wouldn't want you to be bored. Talk
about something else.

VIDAL I don't want to talk.
(*He looks into her eyes*)

CHARITY (*Falling under his spell*) What *do* you want
to do?

VIDAL (*Soulfully*) I want to dance.
(*She joins him on the floor. They start to dance
and she steps on his foot*)

CHARITY Oh, I'm sorry. I'm a little woozy—I haven't eaten

since breakfast. Would you be kind enough to hold out your arms?

VIDAL   Why?

CHARITY   I'm going to faint.
    (*And she faints in his arms. He picks her up*)

FIRST DANCER   She's passed out!

SECOND DANCER   Somebody get some ammonia.

THIRD DANCER   Rub her wrists.

FOURTH DANCER   Loosen her collar.

FIFTH DANCER   Give her air. Give her air.
    (*There is general agreement*)

SIXTH DANCER   Put her down.

OTHER DANCERS   Yeah, lay her down.

VIDAL (*Looks around*)   Where?

CHARITY (*Opens her eyes eagerly*)   Your apartment!
    (*He carries her from the night club into his apartment*)

End of scene

VITTORIO VIDAL's *apartment. A light has remained on* CHARITY *and* VIDAL *as he carries her in. The room then lights up.* VIDAL's *apartment is large and in good taste. We are in a combination bedroom, sitting-room and dressing room.*

His bed is an oversized chaise covered with a fur throw and a great many pillows (that possibly spell out VIDAL *on the bed). There is a huge wardrobe closet with sliding doors and a smaller supplementary closet. In one corner of the room is a teacart which has been converted into an elaborate, well-stocked bar. There is a hi-fi. The overall effect is extravagance and sensualism.*

The music of the new scene has drifted away when the new set has come into place. VIDAL's MAN *is chilling some champagne when* VIDAL *carries* CHARITY *in.*

VIDAL   My apartment.

CHARITY   Hmm, cozy!

VIDAL   Good evening, Manfred.

MANFRED   Good evening, sir. (*Extends a hand toward* CHARITY *in* VIDAL's *arms*) I've laid out a small supper.

VIDAL   Thank you, Manfred. Were there any calls for me?

MANFRED   No, sir. No calls.

CHARITY   And let's keep it that way.

VIDAL   Good night, Manfred.

MANFRED   Good night, sir. Good night, ma'am.

CHARITY   Good night, Manny. (MANFRED *exits*) He's

sweet. You're lucky to have someone worried about you all the time.

VIDAL I'm worried about you right this minute. Do you want to lie down now?

CHARITY (*Coyly*) It's your bed; whatever you say.

VIDAL (*Puts her down on the bed*) I say you should have something to eat. (*Crosses to the table with the food*) What would you like? Chicken? Ham? Turkey? Genoa salami?

CHARITY Isn't that funny? The minute Manny went to bed, I wasn't hungry any more.

VIDAL (*Taking off his jacket and crossing to the closet*) You're a funny girl.

CHARITY Yeah? Is that good or bad?

VIDAL It's good, very good.

CHARITY (*Gets up, smiling*) No kidding? Hey, keep talking.

VIDAL (*Puts on his robe*) You know, I just realized. I don't know a thing about you.

CHARITY Oh, I could tell you everything about me. Who I am and what I do, but it would be a waste of time 'cause I'm gonna lie.

VIDAL (*Crossing to the champagne bottle*) Why would you lie?

CHARITY Because I want to impress you and if I told you what I really did you wouldn't be very impressed.

VIDAL Let me be the judge of that. What do you do?

CHARITY I'm a dance hall hostess.

33

VIDAL Oh.

CHARITY You see. You shoulda let me lie. I was gonna be an Assistant Dental Technician.

VIDAL (*Opening the champagne*) That doesn't sound very impressive.

CHARITY It is to a dance hall hostess.

VIDAL *You're* the one who doesn't seem very impressed. (*Pours champagne*) Why did you ever take a job like that?

CHARITY I don't know. Fickle finger of fate, I guess.

VIDAL What?

CHARITY Fickle finger of fate. Don't you know what that means?

VIDAL Yes, I think so.

CHARITY I don't. Not really. But so many things seem to happen to me and I don't know why or how. People always ask me, "Why did you take up with that guy?" or, "How did you wind up in that joint?" I got so embarrassed always saying, "I don't know." But it was the truth. I don't. (*She spits out an olive pit*) Scusi. But I guess you're supposed to know *why* you do things or *how* you wind up in places. (*She shrugs*) Anyway, now when anyone asks me why or how I just say, "Fickle finger of fate," and I don't get embarrassed any more.

VIDAL I think you just like saying it.

CHARITY (*Delighted*) I think you're right. Fickle finger of fate . . . Fickle finger of fate. (*She laughs*) Feels good. It cools the mouth. You wanna try it?

VIDAL All right. Fickle finger of fate.

34

CHARITY You like it?

VIDAL Very nice.

CHARITY I got lots of phrases I like to say, even when they don't exactly fit. Like if some wise-acre at the Fan-Dango says to me something fresh or something dirty and I just can't think quick enough to answer, I like to say, "Up yours."

VIDAL (*A little surprised*) You do?

CHARITY Oh, yeah. That's a good one. Fits almost any question. Of course I wouldn't say it to a nice refined gentleman like you. I mean it wouldn't be right. You say to me, "Why did you ever take a job like a dance hall hostess?" And then I say, "Up yours." It just isn't nice. But I can say "Fickle finger of fate," can't I?

VIDAL (*Laughs*) You certainly can. (*Hands her a glass*) Here. Let's drink to it.

CHARITY Okay.

VIDAL (*Holds up his glass*) To the fickle finger—

CHARITY —of fate.
(*They click glasses*)

VIDAL Bottoms up!

CHARITY Up yours! (*Puts her hand quickly over her mouth*) It just slipped out.

VIDAL (*Laughs*) You're wonderful. You're really wonderful.

CHARITY Me? Me wonderful? Wow! Hey, that's really something coming from Vittorio Vidal.

VIDAL (*Pours more for himself*) What makes you think Vittorio Vidal is so special?

35

CHARITY   Are you kidding? Have you ever seen you in the movies?

VIDAL   (*Sits, holding his glass and the bottle*)   Not recently. If nothing else, I have good taste.

CHARITY   Well, you don't know what you're missing. You should've seen the picture you made with Monica Monicelli.

>   (*She pronounces it "Munn-icker Munn-ickerlee"*)

VIDAL   (*Corrects her pronunciation*)   Monica Monicelli.

CHARITY   Yeah. There was this scene. I couldn't see it too good 'cause it was very foggy. Anyway, you had just finished making wild love to her—which is why I think it was foggy—and she started to cry, like this (*She cries*) . . . "Mario. Mario." And then do you remember what you did?

VIDAL   Fortunately, no.

CHARITY   I will as long as I live. You bent down and kissed every one of her fingers. From pinky to thumb. And then you said—and I remember every word exactly—you said, "Without love, life has no purpose!" Wow! Did that ever hit home. (*Pounds her chest*) You got me right where I live. I went through the whole picture and six Milky Ways just to hear that line again. "Without love, life has no purpose."

VIDAL   Is that what you believe?

CHARITY   Oh sure. Don't you? Doesn't everybody?

VIDAL   Why? Why do you believe in love?

CHARITY   (*Shrugs*)   I don't know. You got to have some religion.

VIDAL   And so your religion is love?

36

CHARITY Well, I'll tell you one thing, I sure go to the church a lot.

VIDAL (*Smiles, shaking his head*) Signorina Valentine, I see you sitting there with my own eyes—but I find it hard to believe you really exist.

CHARITY I don't believe I'm here either. Say, do you think I could have a personally autographed picture? Just so I could prove it to myself tomorrow.

VIDAL (*Gets up and goes to the dresser*) It's the least I can do. (*Opens a drawer, taking out pictures*) With mustache or without?

CHARITY Without.

VIDAL (*Starts to write*) "For?"

CHARITY Charity . . .

VIDAL "For Charity . . ."
(*He looks at her to continue*)

CHARITY (*Dictating*) "who was with me in my apartment tonight" (*He smiles and writes*) . . . "alone!" (*He writes*) "I swear it." (*Dictating*) . . . "Vittorio Vi—"

VIDAL I know the rest. (*Hands her the picture*) Eccola.

CHARITY Thanks. (*Takes the picture and looks at it proudly*) You move right into my locker tomorrow night. Gee, what a night for me. Champagne, dancing, personally autographed picture—but it may not be enough.

VIDAL For what?

CHARITY To prove to my girl friends I was really here. Say, do you think I could have some small article of personal apparel? You know, like a tie, a handkerchief, an old camel's hair coat, anything.

37

VIDAL   I'll get something for you now. (*Starts for the door, then stops*) You won't leave?

CHARITY   Hurricane Hazel could strike, I'm not moving. (*He smiles and nods at her and exits.* CHARITY, *very contented with herself, looks around the room. The music starts*) The girls at the Ballroom would never believe me in a million years. (*She sings and dances*)
    If they could see me now,
    That little gang of mine—
    I'm eating fancy chow
    And drinking fancy wine—
    I'd like those stumble-bums
    To see for a fact
    The kind of top-drawer first-rate
    Chums I attract!
    All I can say is *wow-*
    Eee, looka where I am!
    Tonight I landed *pow!*
    Right in a pot of jam!
    What a set-up! Holy cow,
    They'd never believe it
    If my friends could see me now!
    They'd never believe it—
    They'd never believe—
        (VIDAL *comes in.* CHARITY *bumps into him and stops her dance*)

VIDAL (*He has a pop-up top hat which he snaps and "pops up"*)   I used this in my first picture, *Million Dollar Lips.*

CHARITY   What a beautiful black thing.

VIDAL   It's a hat. (*Opens it*) *Eccola.* (*Smiles*) Wait. There's some more.
    (*He exits*)

38

CHARITY (*Singing*)
    If they could see me now,
    My little dusty group,
    Traipsing 'round this
    Million-dollar chicken coop!
    I'd hear those thrift-shop cats say:
    "Brother! Get her!"
    Draped on a bedspread made from
    Three kinds of fur!
    All I can say is: "Wow!"
    Wait till the riff and raff
    See just exactly how
    He signed this autograph!
    What a build-up! Holy cow,
    They'd never believe it
    If my friends could see me now!
    (*At the end of the second chorus and her dance,*
    CHARITY *is bouncing on the bed. She is caught, em-*
    barrassed, by VIDAL's *return. He has a walking*
    stick. CHARITY *jumps off the bed*)
Sealy Posturpedic.
    (*Patting the mattress*)

VIDAL   I used this in *The Dancing Spy*. It's yours.

CHARITY   I couldn't.

VIDAL   You must.

CHARITY   I can't.

VIDAL   I insist.

CHARITY   I'll take it.
    (*She takes the stick*)

VIDAL   Wait. There's more.
    (*He goes back into the other room*)

CHARITY *Ciao*, Vittorio, baby. (CHARITY, *with walking stick and top hat, sings*)

> If they could see me now,
> Alone with Mr. V!
> Who's waiting on me like he was a maitre d'!
> I hear my buddies saying:
> "Crazy! What gives?
> Tonight she's living like the other half lives!"
> To think the highest-brow,
> Which I must say is he,
> Should pick the lowest-brow,
> Which there's no doubt is me,
> What a step up! Holy cow!
> They'd never believe it
> If my friends could see me now!
>> (*She dances. Near the end of her dance, she sings again*)
> They'd never believe it
> They'd never believe it
> If my friends could see me now.
>> (*She dances*)
> Hi, girls—it's me—Charity!
>> (*At the end of her song, VIDAL comes out again. CHARITY has finished the last chorus on one knee with arms outstretched a la Al Jolson. VIDAL catches her like this*)

VIDAL Miss Charity Valentine. Come here. Please. (*He takes her to the side*) In all my possessions, I find I have nothing that truly expresses my warm feeling for you. So I ask you, please to accept this.

> (*He gives her a light, simple, affectionate kiss on her forehead. She is overwhelmed*)

CHARITY I accept. And may I say I never received a gift that came in such a gorgeous package.

VIDAL And now . . .

40

Gwen Verdon, Helen Gallagher and Thelma Oliver—as CHARITY, NICKIE and
HELENE—sing "There's Gotta Be Something Better Than This."

CHARITY Yes? And now?

VIDAL And now—shall we have dinner?

CHARITY Mr. Vidal, you've been so nice to me. Is there any way—that I can return the favor?

VIDAL I don't understand.

CHARITY I mean—is there *anything* I can do? I mean, *anything* you want me to do? Am I making myself clear?

VIDAL Perfectly. Now shall we have dinner?

CHARITY I'm not making myself clear. Mr. Vidal, you've been so nice to me, is there *anything* . . . ?

VIDAL (*Takes her hand*) I *know* what you mean.

CHARITY Oh. Okay. Let's have dinner. Of course, later on if you should change your mind about "you know," well, what the hell—you know what I mean? (*He smiles and nods*) You see, I know the heartbreak you're going through. I too have been to the well and have come up with an empty bucket.

VIDAL You mean Ursala?

CHARITY You're nuts about her, right?

VIDAL Ha! I haven't given her a thought all night.

CHARITY Yeah, she's got you ga ga. I can tell by the way you say her name. You got little violins in your voice. (*She demonstrates with little violins in her voice*) Ursala! Ursala!

VIDAL Nonsense!
        (MANFRED *rushes in*)

MANFRED Sir, Miss March is at the door.

VIDAL (*With violins in his voice*) Ursala?

CHARITY See what I mean?

VIDAL (*To* MANFRED) Get rid of her. Tell her I'm not in.

MANFRED I did, sir, but she insists on seeing you anyway.

VIDAL (*To* CHARITY) Why? Why does she torture me like this?

CHARITY (*Shrugs*) Fickle finger of fate, I guess.

URSALA (*Offstage*) Vittorio, let me in. I must talk to you.

VIDAL Talk? You mean scream, don't you? (*To* CHARITY) What should I do? Help me.

CHARITY Be firm. Be strong. Be a man!

VIDAL (*Firmly*) Yes!

URSALA (*Pleading*) Please, Vittorio, I beg of you. Please.

VIDAL No.

URSALA Please.

VIDAL No.

URSALA Please.

CHARITY I can't stand it. Let her in.

VIDAL Yes, let her in.
(MANFRED *starts for the door*)

CHARITY (*To* MANFRED) Wait a minute. (*To* VIDAL) I'd better get in the closet.

VIDAL Why?

CHARITY If she can't see me, I wasn't here.

URSALA Please.

VIDAL Thank you very much. You're wonderful. (*He opens the door of the closet.* CHARITY *jumps into the closet and shuts the door*) All right, Manfred.

42

(*The closet door opens again and* CHARITY *sticks her head out*)

CHARITY   Hey! This is just like that French picture you made, *Six in a Bed*.
(*She shuts the door herself*)

MANFRED   Can I open it, sir?
(VIDAL *nods but—the closet door opens again*)

CHARITY   Oh! Hold it! (*She gets out, rushes to the food table and quickly makes herself a fat sandwich. Then she rushes back toward the closet*) . . . If you get a chance, I'd love a cold beer.
(*She gets back into the closet and* VIDAL *shuts the door and nods to* MANFRED, *who crosses and opens the other door.*

The audience can now see CHARITY *in the closet. We are in a split set. The closet is very small. Three or four coats are hanging up, along with several garment bags, the kind with a zipper up the side, and other assorted items.* MANFRED *opens the door and* URSALA *rushes in*)

URSALA   What's going on? I heard voices. Who are you talking to?

VIDAL   Is that why you came back? To accuse me again? (MANFRED *tiptoes out*) All right, it's that girl I picked up in front of the club. She's been with me all night and she's in that closet right now. (*He points to the closet*) Go on. Look for yourself.
(CHARITY *tries to hide behind a sports jacket*)

URSALA   All right, I will. (*She walks to the closet and opens it as* CHARITY *tries to hide further behind the jacket. But* URSALA *does not look in*) What's wrong with me? Thinking you could stoop so low as to hide a girl in a closet. (*She closes the door*) Oh, Vittorio, forgive me, forgive me. (CHARITY *takes the sleeve of the sports jacket and wipes her brow*) I don't know what comes over me. The thought of you with another girl drives me insane. (CHARITY *puts her ear right next to the door so she can hear better*) I try to fight it, Vittorio, but I can't. Why do I torture myself? *Why? Why? Why?* (*On the final "Why," she pounds on the closet door with her fist.* CHARITY, *with her head on the other side of the door, holds her head as though she's just been kicked by a horse*) Oh, Vittorio, if I knew you really cared, I'd forgive you anything.

VIDAL   Care? *Cara mia,* do you think a man as passionate as me could suddenly stop caring?
(VIDAL *has edged to the closet with a bottle of beer. He surreptitiously opens the door and passes it to* CHARITY, *who drinks a long draught*)

URSALA (*Smiles*)   Oh, Vittorio, and to think I was even jealous of that little nothing you picked up tonight.
(CHARITY *reacts and mouths, "Nothing?" Then she pantomimes "Up yours" to* URSALA)

VIDAL   Why do we say the things we do? Why do we torture each other like this?

URSALA   Because I'm an immature, foolish child, that's why.
(CHARITY *nods*)

VIDAL   It's my vanity. My stupid, egotistical vanity.
(CHARITY *shakes her head, "No"*)

URSALA   No, darling, it's my fault. It's all mine.
(CHARITY *nods*)

VIDAL   I don't know any more. I just don't know *whose* fault it is.
(CHARITY *points to* URSALA *and mouths silently, "Hers!"*)

44

URSALA I never want to be away from you. Ever again.

VIDAL It's no good without you, Ursala. No good at all.

URSALA Without you, Vittorio, there is no love.

VIDAL (*Postures*) And without love, life has no purpose!
(*He says it much the way* CHARITY *did before.* CHARITY,
*in the closet, nods as if to say, "Oh, well," then lights a
cigarette. The orchestra starts to play.* CHARITY *looks
through the keyhole again*) Ursala, Ursala. My darling.

URSALA Oh, Vittorio, Vittorio.
        (*They kiss.* CHARITY *watches the kiss, which is
        a long one, and yawns.* VIDAL *sings to* URSALA)

VIDAL
        Please don't go my love.
        I'm frightened of
        Too many tomorrows
        Around this haunted place.
        If I set you free,
        What's left for me?
        Too many tomorrows
        I simply cannot face.
        Those passionate words we find
        To grieve each other
        Do not mean
        We'd leave each other.

        So come fill my arms
        And we'll forget
        The meaningless sorrows
        Each time we say we're through.
        Darling, can't you see,
        There can't ever be
        Too many tomorrows
        If you stay with me.
            (*During the song, smoke starts to fill up the closet.*
            CHARITY, *afraid that it will seep out through the*

45

keyhole, puts her hand over the keyhole, but that will not do. Neither will waving the smoke away. She tries to hold in the next puff, letting a little dribble out of the side of her mouth.

    She looks for a place to hide the smoke. She sees a garment bag. She unzips it and exhales into the garment bag. She zips it up. Another puff. Another zip when she exhales. She zips it up)

VIDAL *(Sings)*
    So come fill my arms
    And we'll forget
    The meaningless sorrows
    Each time we say we're through.
    Darling, can't you see,
    There can never be
    Too many tomorrows
    If you stay with me.
    (He lies on the bed with URSALA—*on half of the bed. A curtain drops, covering their side of the bed. From behind the curtain)*

VIDAL'S VOICE   Ursala . . . my angel . . . my darling . . . my sweet . . .

URSALA'S VOICE   Oh, Vittorio! You're *not* a fading Romeo, Vittorio. You're not . . .
    *(*CHARITY *cannot contain herself and looks through the keyhole again—with growing appreciation)*

CHARITY *(She whistles appreciatively)*   Gee, talk about your foreign movies!
    (She sings the line: "If my friends could see me now." The lights fade on the other half of the bed and the curtain falls around it.

    The lights have faded to blackout. A sign appears. It reads: "A NEW DAY." It disappears.

    The lights come up slowly to reveal the split set

again. It is dawn. URSALA *is asleep on the bed under the fur, smiling.* CHARITY *is asleep standing up in the closet, looking haggard.* VIDAL *tiptoes to the closet, opens it and* CHARITY *falls out. He catches her)*

CHARITY   Wha—?

VIDAL   Shh. (*He whispers*) Are you all right?

CHARITY (*Painfully smiles. She holds her back and whispers*)   It's like those little roomettes that go to Florida. (*She gets out of the closet with his help*)

VIDAL (*Whispers*)   Thank you very much for everything —and if there's anything I can do . . .

CHARITY (*Takes out his autographed picture*)   You already did it.
     (*She starts to tiptoe out past* URSALA. URSALA *extends an arm through the curtain and calls out sexily*)

URSALA   Vittorio!
     (VIDAL *crosses back and kisses* URSALA's *extended hand.* CHARITY *watches enthralled.* VIDAL *propels her to the door*)

CHARITY (*Whispers*)   I've enjoyed your pictures, but in person!

VIDAL   You mean, you watched? *Everything?*
     (CHARITY *gives him a wink and an "O.K., Charlie" sign*)

CHARITY   *Ciao!*
     (*She exits*)

VITTORIO   *Ciao!*

End of scene

SCENE 7

During the scene change CHARITY *dances around the stage. She sings:*

CHARITY

> They'll never believe me
> If they could see me now,
> That little dusty group . . .
>> (*The lights come up on the hostess room of the Fan-Dango Ballroom.*
>>
>> BETSY, HELENE *and* NICKIE *are getting dressed.* CHARITY *walks in very excited, still clutching the cane and top hat*)

CHARITY . . . and then I left his apartment at five o'clock in the morning and went home. And you know how I got back to Ninety-fourth Street? I flew! My feet never once touched the ground.

HELENE (*Putting on eye make-up*) . . . Yeah, well, you keep smoking them funny little cigarettes, you bound to do a little flying.

CHARITY You don't believe me? You don't believe I spent the night with Vittorio Vidal!

NICKIE You swear?

CHARITY I swear.

NICKIE On your mother's life?

CHARITY On my mother's life.

NICKIE (*To* SISSIE) Call up and find out how her mother is.

48

CHARITY (*Shows her the mementos*) Here. He gave me these. His hat and his cane. They're mementos of our evening together.

BETSY Is that all he gave you?
    (CHARITY *nods*)

NICKIE Honey, if I was you I'd pass the hat and beat myself to death with the cane 'cause you are dumb.

CHARITY But you don't know what happened.

NICKIE Forget it. What you do in bed is your business.

CHARITY I wasn't in bed; I was in the closet.

NICKIE To each his own.

BETSY You coulda had a mink coat.
    (*She exits*)

CHARITY Why would he give me a mink coat?

HELENE Well, if you're gonna mess with the details you ain't gonna get no results.

NICKIE A hat and a cane. If it was me, I woulda walked outta there with my own beauty parlor.

HELENE Now you'll never get out of here.

NICKIE Baby, you're stuck. Stuck just like the rest of us.

HELENE Yeah, and it ain't no use flappin' your wings, 'cause we are caught in the fly paper of life.
    (*They all sit gloomily in silence for a moment. After the pause*)

NICKIE . . . Not me.
    (*They look at her*)

HELENE What'd you say?

NICKIE (*Determined*)   I said not me. I'm not gonna spend the next forty years in the Fan-Dango Ballroom. I'm not gonna become the world's first little old taxi dancer. I'm gettin' out.

HELENE   Out. What a beautiful word—

NICKIE (*Singing*)
There's gotta be something better than this.
There's gotta be something better to do.
And when I find me something better to do,
I'm gonna get up; I'm gonna get out; I'm gonna get up,
    get out and do it!

There's gotta be some respectable trade.
There's gotta be something easy to learn.
And if I find me something a half-wit can learn,
I'm gonna get up; I'm gonna get out; I'm gonna get up,
    get out and learn it!

All these jokers, how I hate them,
With the groping, grabbing, clutching, clinching,
Strangling, handling, fumbling, pinching . . .
    (*Speaking*)
Phooey. (*Singing*)
There's gotta be some life cleaner than this.
There's gotta be some good reason to live.
And when I find me some kind of life I can live,
I'm gonna get up; I'm gonna get out; I'm gonna get up,
    get out and live it!*

RECEPTIONIST   I got it! I got it! I'm gonna be a receptionist in one of those glass office buildings like Lever Brothers. No, Seagrams. Nine to five! I'm gonna have my own typewriter—Underwood! Water coolers—office parties—coffee breaks!

CHARITY and HELENE   Ooh!

RECEPTIONIST (*Sings*)
>When I sit at my desk on the forty-first floor,
>In my copy of a copy of a copy of Dior,
>I'll receive big tycoons and I'll point to a chair.
>I'll say "Honey, while you're waiting, how would you
>>like to put it down over there."
>(*The girls hug each other*)
>
>There's gotta be something better than this.
>There's gotta be something better to do.
>And when I find me something better to do,
>I'm gonna get up; I'm gonna get out; I'm gonna get up,
>>get out and do it!
>
>Typewriter! Cover off!
>(*Pantomime*)
>
>And if I find me something a half-wit can learn
>I'm gonna get up; I'm gonna get out; I'm gonna get up,
>>get out and learn it!

HELENE   Me too—me too! I'm gonna get outta here and go right to the top! I am gonna be a hat check girl. At Sardi's East. I'll wear one of those cute lil' black numbers —cut up to there and down to there. All those hats comin' in—derbies—homburgs—and that cute little checked one with the skinny brim—and the feather. (*She sings*)
>Check your hat, sir? Check your coat, sir? Check your
>>vest, sir? Check your pants?
>Check your socks, sir? Check your shoes, sir? I can
>>hold them while you dance!

Check your eyes, sir? Check your ears, sir? Check
and see if you are free.
How about it; after hours I'll check you and you
check me!
(*She hugs the other girls and dances*)

CHARITY Me too!

HELENE and NICKIE What?

CHARITY I'm getting out too!

NICKIE But, baby—what can you do?

CHARITY I dunno. Just get me out of here and I'll figure it
out later. (*She sings*)
There's gotta be some life cleaner than this.
There's gotta be some good reason to live.
And when I find me some kind of life I can live,
I'm gonna get up; I'm gonna get out; I'm gonna get up,
get out and live it!
(*She dances*)

And when I find me some kind of life I can live,
I'm gonna get up; I'm gonna get out; I'm gonna get up,
get out and live—
And live it!
(*After the song,* HERMAN *the manager enters*)

HERMAN Ladies, they have just announced the winners
of the 1966 Irish Sweepstakes. And since none of you
ladies are among the winners, get your ass out there.

CHARITY (*Angrily, to* HERMAN) In the *first* place, watch
your language! And in the *second* place, we're not so
sure we're comin' out.

HERMAN I can always find someone else.

HELENE *That's* the third place. I'm comin', Herman.

(HELENE *follows* HERMAN *out.* NICKIE *starts out too*)

CHARITY   Wait a minute. What happened to all those wonderful plans we just had?

NICKIE (*Forlornly*)   Yeah, whatever happened to them? (*They both exit, leaving* CHARITY)

CHARITY (*Shouting after them*)   Well, I'm not giving up without a fight. (*She picks up the hat and cane and looks at it. A sign appears: "A BIG DECISION"*) . . . I've got to get out of this dump. Go to new places . . . meet new people. All I need is a different background . . . a little culture . . . a little refinement . . . and I know just the place to get it . . .

(*There is a blackout on* CHARITY *as a new sign immediately lights up: "THE 92ND STREET 'Y'"*)

End of scene

The Ninety-second Street "Y." The lights come up on one corner of the stage. There is a booth with a GIRL sitting behind it. Over the booth there is an "Information" sign. The OLD MAID approaches the booth.

GIRL (*To the* OLD MAID) Yes? Can I help you?

OLD MAID (*Whispers*) I'm looking for sex in the later stages of marriage.

GIRL I beg your pardon?

OLD MAID (*Whispers*) The lecture. "On Sex in the Later Stages of Marriage."

GIRL Oh. Lecture Hall Two.

OLD MAID Thank you. (*Starts to go and then stops*) Is it all right if you're not married?

GIRL It's even better.
(*The* SECOND WOMAN *approaches*)

SECOND WOMAN Excuse me. Could you tell me where Norman Mailer is reading his poetry tonight?

GIRL At home. Nobody showed up.

SECOND WOMAN Oh, dear.
(*She exits.* CHARITY *enters and goes to the booth*)

CHARITY Hello. I'm interested in joining a cultural group.

GIRL Certainly. Are you a member of the "Y"?
(*A shy, attractive man in his mid-thirties,* OSCAR, *approaches the booth*)

OSCAR Excuse me, what room is the Free Thought in Action Society?

GIRL One moment. This young lady was here first.

OSCAR I'm sorry, but the class starts at eight and it's eight-fifteen now—

GIRL (*Coldly*) When I'm through.

OSCAR (*Meekly*) When you're through. Yes.
(*He looks at* CHARITY *and smiles with embarrassment. She smiles back. After all, he does have a nice face*)

GIRL (*To* CHARITY) Now at nine o'clock we have Dr. Sidney Greenwald. Would you be interested in the Psychologists' Workshop?

CHARITY No. I'm really not very good with my hands.

OSCAR I, er, really hate to interrupt, but I'm going to be very late and—

CHARITY He's going to be very late.

GIRL (*Annoyed*) Oh, all right. Room 603.

OSCAR 603. Thank you very much. Thank you. (*To* CHARITY) And thank you—603 . . .
(CHARITY *smiles at him as he goes off. She continues to look after him*)

CHARITY (*To* GIRL) What kind of group is that, Free Thought in Action?

GIRL It's a self-analytical discussion group. People are prodded into saying anything that comes into their minds—under the careful supervision of a medical student. It can be very dangerous.

CHARITY (*Still looking after* OSCAR) Hmm, I think I'll

55

take a crack at that. Room 603? (CHARITY *follows* OSCAR *off. The lights come up on a small, self-service elevator. It is big enough to accommodate only three or four people at the most. It is constructed so as to give the illusion of being enclosed, but of course the interior of the elevator is in full view of the audience at all times. The elevator door opens and three people push out as* OSCAR *waits and then gets in.* CHARITY *comes running up, calling*) Going up! Going up! (OSCAR *holds the door back to keep it from closing on* CHARITY *and she gets in.* OSCAR *takes off his hat*) Thank you.

OSCAR (*About to press the button*)   I'm going to six.

CHARITY (*Smiles*)   Likewise.
(OSCAR *smiles back and presses the button. The elevator door closes and they ride up silently.* OSCAR, *with his hat in his hand, stares quietly ahead.* CHARITY *does too, but then slyly glances his way, then looks back out at nothing. Suddenly, they both jerk forward and we get the impression that the elevator has come to a sudden stop—but the door does not open. They are obviously between floors. It is plain to see from the blanched expression on* OSCAR's *face that he is not comfortable in this situation*)

OSCAR (*Nervously*)   What was that?

CHARITY   We stopped. Press the button. It'll start right in again.
(OSCAR *quickly presses the button but nothing happens. He presses it again and again. The elevator doesn't move*)

OSCAR   Something's wrong. We're stuck.

CHARITY (*Cheerfully*)   These old elevators. You never can trust them.

56

OSCAR (*Nervously wipes his forehead*) Oh, boy.

CHARITY I had a friend who was stuck in one for eight hours. With two German shepherds and a delivery boy.

OSCAR (*Is getting extremely tense. He loosens his tie*) It's kind of stuffy in here, isn't it? Isn't it stuffy?

CHARITY You think so?

OSCAR (*Unbuttons his top shirt button*) . . . You want to try pressing the buttons?

CHARITY No, that's all right. I'm sure you pressed them very well.

OSCAR (*Nods*) I did. I pressed them very well. I gave them a very good press. Soooo, I guess we're stuck.

CHARITY I guess so . . . (*She looks at the Inspector's Card on the wall and reads*) "Maximum weight in pounds, one thousand three hundred."

OSCAR (*Looks at her*) What do you weigh?

CHARITY A hundred and twenty-eight.

OSCAR We're all right.

CHARITY Sure.

OSCAR Yeah, we're fine. Fine. We're just stuck in the old elevator . . .
    (*He forces a little laugh*)

CHARITY Are you all right?

OSCAR (*Quickly*) Me? Me? Yes. Yes. Fine. Yes, I'm fine. Fine. Just have to get used to it, that's all. It's my first time *trapped* in an elevator. Trapped, trapped, trapped.

CHARITY Hey! You don't have claustrophobia, do you?

57

OSCAR (*Scoffing*) Oh, no. No. No, nothing like that. Claustrophobia? No, I just don't like to be in small, tight places that I can't get out of.

CHARITY Oh, I understand. I used to have that with zippers. I was once trapped in a dress for twenty minutes. I screamed all over Orbach's.

OSCAR That's claustrophobia. You've got to watch out for that. No, I can handle this because I know we'll get out of here in a couple of minutes.

CHARITY Sure we will.

OSCAR (*Hopefully*) You really think so?

CHARITY I do. I really do.

OSCAR But if you thought we were really trapped in here, what would you say?

CHARITY But we're not trapped.

OSCAR But if you thought we were, what would you say?

CHARITY I'd say we were really trapped.

OSCAR Oh, my God, I knew it; I knew it!

CHARITY But we're not. You really shouldn't get so excited.

OSCAR Isn't this awful? I never act this way. I'm really a very calm person. Highly organized. I can promise you that if it really comes down to it, you can depend on me. You understand that?

CHARITY I do.

OSCAR I just hope it doesn't come down to it. Maybe I should yell for help?

CHARITY Why not?

OSCAR *I'm* all right, you understand. But I know that you suffer from claustrophobia and I realize you're very uncomfortable and I wouldn't want you to be stuck in here any longer than I have to be. Help! Help! Hel—
(CHARITY *touches him. He jumps violently*)

CHARITY My name is Charity Valentine. Hey, you're shaking.

OSCAR All over.

CHARITY Let me rub your wrists.
(*She rubs them*)

OSCAR You know what I feel like doing now? What my impulse is? To take off my clothes.

CHARITY Oh, well, I don't think that would do much good.

OSCAR (*Snappy*) You'd think they'd have a telephone in here, wouldn't you? Never again. I'll never go in an elevator without a telephone. I'll always check for a telephone.

CHARITY We really should change the subject. You wanna play actors and actresses?

OSCAR (*Yells down*) Hey, come on. We don't think it's funny any more.

CHARITY Try not to think of it. Play the game. Awright, what actress was in *Sabrina Fair*? You get three guesses. Ready? Julie Andrews—

OSCAR I don't want to play. I really don't feel like playing. It's a stupid game for two people trapped in an elevator to play. No offense.

CHARITY I'm just trying to pass the time.

59

OSCAR   If I could just get out for a few minutes. Just a few minutes outside and I'd be all right. Then I'd come back inside.

CHARITY   The best thing to do is to keep talking. Then you won't think about it. What's your name? (OSCAR *looks blank*) Your name? What's your name? You know, like Frank, Harry, Sidney, Bruce. That's a name.

OSCAR   Oh, Oscar. My name is Oscar. Whoo, it's stuffy. Stuffy, stuffy, stuffy.

CHARITY   Now, let's keep our clothes on, Oscar. What's your second name?

OSCAR   My what?

CHARITY   Your second name. Don't you have a second name?

OSCAR   No, I don't think so.

CHARITY   Sure you do. Like Oscar Minetti or Oscar Greenspan.

OSCAR   Greenspan—no, Lindquist. Oscar Lindquist. Look how quickly I'm breathing. You notice how quickly I'm breathing? What is that? What is that quick breathing?

CHARITY   That's quick breathing. Don't think about it. Where do you live?

OSCAR   Who?

CHARITY   You! You! Where do you live?

OSCAR   In an elevator.

CHARITY   No, you don't, Oscar. You live in a house.

OSCAR   Oh. Yes. 411 East Seventy-fourth Street. I gotta stop this breathing. I'm gonna use up all the air.

CHARITY   We got plenty, Oscar. Now keep talking. How old are you? Where do you work?

OSCAR   Heh? Yeah. Yeah. I work at thirty-eight years old— and I was a tax accountant for Gallagher and Perlmutter on my last birthday. Oh, boy, that's very quick breathing.

CHARITY   Keep talking. Oscar, what else?

OSCAR   It's not fair. You should breathe some of the air.

CHARITY   Are you married, Oscar? Do you have a wife?

OSCAR   What?

CHARITY   Married? Married? (*Losing control*) For God's sakes, are you *married*?

OSCAR   No. No, I'm not married.

CHARITY   (*Big smile*) Oh, Oscar. You're gonna be all right.

OSCAR   Don't leave me.

CHARITY   Oh—I won't leave you. I'm gonna stay right here in the elevator with you. And you're gonna be all right, Oscar, because I'm gonna help you . . .

OSCAR   How? What should I do?

CHARITY   Just do what I do. (*She sings*)
When I'm so jittery my knees buckle,
Ice water tickles my spine,
I'm trapped like a butterfly in a net,
Then I say to myself:
"I'm the bravest individual I have ever met!"
I chew my fingernails to the knuckle,
Those teeth that chatter are mine.
So I stop and light up a cigarette,
And I say to myself:

"I'm the bravest individual I have ever met!"
This game makes very good sense;
I get results.

OSCAR

Isn't that great?

CHARITY

Get back my confidence and an even pulse—
Seventy-eight—
So when I panic and feel each day
I've come to the end of the line,
Then I say that fear hasn't licked me yet!
I keep telling myself:
"I'm the bravest individual I have ever met!"

OSCAR (*Excited*) Good. Listen, I have an idea. What do
you think of this? Climbing out the top of the elevator,
shimmying up the cable and forcing the door open on
the floor above.

CHARITY I think it could work, Oscar, but gee, it sounds
a little dangerous.

OSCAR Then don't try it. Stay here with me. (*He sings*)
Funny, but suddenly I can't swallow—
I think I'm going to die;
Sometimes, if you pardon the word, I sweat!

CHARITY

Then you say to yourself:

BOTH

"I'm the bravest individual I have ever met!"

OSCAR

"I'm the bravest individual I have ever met!"
Your game makes very good sense;
I get results!

CHARITY

    Isn't that fine!

OSCAR

    Got back my confidence and an even pulse!
       (*He touches his wrist*)
    A hundred and nine!

CHARITY

    So when you panic and think each day
    You'll fail at whatever you try—

OSCAR

    I just say that fear hasn't licked me yet!

CHARITY

    And keep telling yourself:

OSCAR

    "I'm the strongest, soundest, stoical,
    Daringest, manliest, most heroical—"

OSCAR and CHARITY

    "I'm the bravest individual I have ever met!"
      (*At the end of the song,* OSCAR's *spirits have been
      raised enormously by* CHARITY's *encouragement*)

OSCAR (*Beaming*) I'm all right. I'm gonna be all right.

CHARITY Of course you are.

OSCAR I think I've got it licked. I've got it under control.

CHARITY Atta boy, Oscar.

OSCAR No matter what happens now, I'm going to be all
right. (*And on that line, the stage is thrust into total
darkness*) What was that?

63

CHARITY (*In the black*)   The lights went out.

(*Suddenly two matches are struck by* CHARITY *and* OSCAR. *As the two matches flicker pathetically in the dark, we hear both of them, in near panic, calling loudly,* "Help!"

A sign appears: "TO BE CONTINUED")

Curtain

John McMartin as OSCAR and Gwen Verdon as CHARITY declare their love for each other.

Act Two

As the curtain rises, the scene is still the "Y." The stage is in darkness except for the two lonely matches that continue to flicker.

A sign appears: "MEANWHILE BACK IN THE ELEVATOR . . ."

We hear the tired, frightened and weakened voice of CHARITY *singing a rather spiritless rendition of "Bravest Individual." During this* OSCAR *is calling weakly, "Help! Help!" At the end of the chorus, the lights suddenly go back on.*

CHARITY (*Excited*) Oh! The lights are on. Press the button, Oscar, press the button!

> (OSCAR *presses the button. The car jerks and slowly begins to descend*)

OSCAR (*Beside himself with joy*) It's moving! It's moving!

CHARITY I told you, Oscar. I told you we'd be all right. (*He is straightening his tie as the elevator car disappears from view. They are down. The doors open and they emerge*) I knew it was just a matter of time.

OSCAR Your big problem, actually, is panic. That's the cause of your greater number of accidents.

MAN (*Waiting at the elevator door, very nasty*) Oh, so you finally came out, heh? I've been ringing for twenty minutes. Don't you have any consideration for other people?

> (*He gets into the elevator and presses the button. The door closes*)

OSCAR Well, I'll see you—around.

CHARITY Yeah. Around.

OSCAR . . . Around where?

CHARITY I don't know. Where are you going?

OSCAR Well, I was going to Group Analysis, but I guess I missed it tonight.

CHARITY (*Worried*) Will you be all right?

OSCAR Oh, yes. It was my last session this week anyway. I'm finished.

CHARITY Oh, good. What was your problem?

OSCAR Well, one of my problems was—that I was painfully shy.

CHARITY And now you're cured?

OSCAR No. I just never had the nerve to bring it up in class. So I quit.

CHARITY Oh. Well, shyness *ain't* one of my problems. If you noticed.

OSCAR Oh, listen, I am not a nut or anything. I mean, after what happened in there; I can assure you, I'm not what I seem to be at all.

CHARITY You seem to be very nice.

OSCAR Oh, well, then I am what I seem to be because that's what I am—very nice. Well, if you're not doing anything now, would you like to come to church with me?

CHARITY (*Suspicious*) What denomination did you have in mind?

OSCAR It's the Rhythm of Life Church. Under the Manhattan Bridge. It was a jazz group in San Francisco and

68

turned into a religion. I hear it's an emotional experience.

CHARITY (*Smiles*) I'm always looking for an emotional experience.

OSCAR Come on. (*About to ring the elevator bell*) We'll walk down.
        (*They start to run off as the elevator appears, then stops with the MAN in it*)

MAN Help! Help!
        (CHARITY *and* OSCAR *laugh and point up*)

BOTH Aha!
        (*There is a blackout. In the black we hear a voice. It is deep and powerful, reverberating and echoing like Moses speaking from the mountain*)

VOICE This is the Rhythm of Life Church. Tonight's sermon is "Retribution and Absolution." And a one and a two and a three . . .

End of scene

The Rhythm of Life Church. This is a garage converted for the evening into a pathetic, makeshift church. If possible, we should see the backs of a few automobiles protruding from the wings.

DADDY

Daddy started out in San Francisco
Tootin' on his trumpet loud and mean.

ASSISTANTS

Suddenly a voice said:
"Go forth, Daddy;
Spread the picture on a wider screen."

DADDY	BONGOISTS
And the voice said: "Daddy	Daddy . . .
There's a million pigeons	Go . . .
Waitin' to be hooked on new religions.	Go . . . go . . . go . . .
Hit the road, Daddy;	Tell . . . them . . .
Leave your common-law wife;	Ev . . . ry . . .
Spread the religion	Thing . . . you . . .
Of the rhythm of life."	Know . . .

GROUP A

And the rhythm of life
Is a powerful beat,
Puts a tingle in your fingers
And a tingle in your feet,
Rhythm in your bedroom,
Rhythm in the street.
Yes, the rhythm of life
Is a powerful beat!

GROUP A	GROUP B
Oh, the rhythm of life	
Is a powerful beat,	To feel the rhythm of life,
Puts a tingle in your fingers	
And a tingle in your feet,	To feel the powerful beat,
Rhythm in your bedroom,	To feel the tingle
Rhythm in the street.	In your fingers,
Yes, the rhythm of life	To feel the tingle
Is a powerful beat!	In your feet.

GROUP A	GROUP B	GROUP C
Oh: the rhythm of life	To feel the	Daddy . . .
Is a powerful beat,	Rhythm of life,	Go . . .
Puts a tingle	To feel the	Go . . . go . . .
In your fingers	Powerful beat,	Go . . .
And a tingle		
In your feet,		
Rhythm in your bedroom,	To feel the tingle	Tell . . .
		them . . .
Rhythm in the street.	In your fingers,	Ev . . . ry . . .
Yes, the rhythm of life	To feel the tingle	Thing . . .
		you . . .
Is a powerful beat!	In your feet.	Know . . .

DADDY

Daddy spread the gospel in Milwaukee,
Took his walkie-talkie to Rocky Ridge.

DADDY and BONGOISTS

Blew his way to Canton, then to Scranton,
Till he landed under the Manhattan Bridge.

GROUP D

Daddy was a new sensation,
Got himself a congregation,
Built up quite an operation
Down below.

With the pie-eyed piper blowing
While the muscatel was flowing,
All the cats were go-go-going
Down below.

GROUP D	GROUP E
Daddy was a new sensation,	Daddy was a new sensation,
Got himself a congregation,	Got himself a congregation,
Built up quite an operation	Built up quite an operation
Down below.	Down below.

GROUP D

With the pie-eyed piper blowing
While the muscatel was flowing,
All the cats were go-go-going
Down below.

GROUP D	GROUP E
Daddy was a new sensation,	With the pie-eyed piper blowing
Got himself a congregation,	While the muscatel was flowing,
Built up quite a reputation	All the cats were go-go-going
Down below.	Down below.

With the pie-eyed piper blowing
While the muscatel was flowing,
All the cats were go-go-going
Down below.

ALL

Flip your wings and fly to Daddy!
Flip your wings and fly to Daddy!
Flip your wings and fly to Daddy!
Fly . . . fly . . . fly to Daddy!

Take a dive and swim to Daddy!
Take a dive and swim to Daddy!
Take a dive and swim to Daddy!
Swim . . . swim . . . swim to Daddy!

Hit the floor and crawl to Daddy!
Hit the floor and crawl to Daddy!
Hit the floor and crawl to Daddy!
Crawl . . . crawl . . . crawl to Daddy!

Do-do-do-do-do-we-do-we-do-we
Do-do-do-do-do-we-do-we-do-we
Do-do-do-do-do-we-do-we-do-we
Do-do-do-do-do-we-do-we-do-we

Do-do-do-do-do-we-do-we-do-we
Do-do-do-do-do-we-do-we-do-we
Do-do-do-do-do-we-do-we-do-we
Do-do-do-do-do-we-do-we-do-we

GROUP A

And the rhythm of life
Is a powerful beat,
Puts a tingle in your fingers
And a tingle in your feet,
Rhythm in your bedroom,
Rhythm in the street.
Yes, the rhythm of life
Is a powerful beat!

GROUP A

And the rhythm of life
Is a powerful beat,
Puts a tingle in your fingers
And a tingle in your feet,
Rhythm in your bedroom,
Rhythm in the street.
Yes, the rhythm of life
Is a powerful beat!

GROUP B

To feel the
Rhythm of life,
To feel the
Powerful beat,
To feel the tingle
In your fingers,
To feel the tingle
In your feet.

GROUP A	GROUP B	GROUP C
And the rhythm of life	To feel the	Daddy . . .
Is a powerful beat,	Rhythm of life,	Go . . .
Puts a tingle In your fingers	To feel the Powerful beat.	Go . . . Go . . .
And a tingle In your feet.		Go . . .
Rhythm in your bedroom,	To feel the tingle	Tell . . . them . . .
Rhythm in the street.	In your fingers	Ev . . . ry . . .
Yes, the rhythm of life	To feel the tingle	Thing . . . you . . .
Is a powerful beat!	In your feet.	Know . . .

ALL

To feel the rhythm of life,
To feel the powerful beat,
To feel the tingle in your fingers,
To feel the tingle in your feet.

74

Flip your wings and fly to Daddy.
Take a dive and swim to Daddy.
Hit the floor and crawl to Daddy.

Daddy, we've got the rhythm of life,
Of life, of life, of life . . .
Yeah . . . yeah . . . yeah . . . man!
   (*All gather around* DADDY BRUBECK *and his two*
   ASSISTANTS *who are standing on oil drums*)

DADDY BRUBECK   This is where it's happening, Baby. The
   Rhythm of Life—Number Seven in the Ten Top Re-
   ligions.

EDDIE   We're gonna climb to Number One, Daddy.

BRUBECK   Time is running out on the big number called
   Life. And we are all coming to the last eight bars. And
   the leader man will soon take us by the hand where we
   will enter the flip side of life called *Eternity*.

HAROLD   Eternity.

EDDIE   The big coffee break in the sky.

BRUBECK   But before we play that final date and pile into
   that big black bus—we got to make our peace.

HAROLD   Make it, Daddy; make it.

BRUBECK   I shall not put my mother and father down.

GROUP   No, Daddy.

BRUBECK   I shall honor my debts, my grievances and my
   alimony.

GROUP   Oh, yeah.

BRUBECK   I shall not falsify my name at the Unemploy-
   ment Bureau.

75

GROUP   Oh, yeah!

BRUBECK   I shall respect my obligations and report each month to the Police.

GROUP   Oh, yeah.

CHARITY (*To* OSCAR)   They're a very devout group, aren't they?

OSCAR   Yes.
>   (*The* GROUP *sings and hums rhythmically*)

BRUBECK   I shall not indulge in the evil marijuana weed commonly known as pot. It is sinful; it is harmful—and it is very expensive . . . (*Sirens and police whistles sound*) And I suggest you dump the goods before the cops arrive.
>   (*The congregation stamps out their cigarettes and there is a mad dash by all to escape*)

End of scene

OSCAR *and* CHARITY *are on a New York street, going cross-town. They are both breathless.*

OSCAR   Gee. I'm sorry about that.

CHARITY   Where do you find places like that?

OSCAR   I'm on a mailing list. It's the Church of the Month Club. (*Looks at her warmly*) Look, will I—may I see you tomorrow night?

CHARITY   Well, it depends what you have in mind. I mean if it's going to be a human sacrifice or something, I really don't—

OSCAR   A movie. A plain, ordinary movie with a happy ending.

CHARITY   (*Smiles*)   I'm nuts about happy endings.
       (*They head toward the subway, joining a crowd of other passengers moving toward the trains*)

OSCAR   I'll pick you up after work. At your office?

CHARITY   (*Nervously*)   What makes you think I work in an office?

OSCAR   It's a hobby of mine. I could look at a person's face and in a second tell what they do. As a matter of fact, I know exactly what *kind* of an office you work in. If I'm wrong, you don't have to keep the date. You work in a bank, right?

CHARITY   (*Smiles*)   You guessed it. First National City, Williamsburg Branch.

OSCAR   I knew it. I'm a great judge of character. How's six o'clock at the bank?

CHARITY   Oh, listen, I wouldn't want you to come all the way out to Williamsburg. Besides, tomorrow we have to take inventory. You know, count all the blotters and the pennies. All that jazz . . . Suppose I meet you in front of the "Y"?

OSCAR   Where?

CHARITY   In front of the "Y."

OSCAR   *Where?*

SUBWAY PASSENGERS   In front of the "Y"!
     (*She steps out of the subway entrance*)

OSCAR (*He moves closer*)   I—I just want to say, I had a very nice time tonight, Charity—I mean, being with you.

CHARITY   So did I, Oscar . . .
     (*They look at each other. There is a pause. A sign appears: "THE FIRST KISS"*)

OSCAR (*Moves closer*)   A very nice time.

CHARITY   That's what I had. A very nice time.

OSCAR   Well, good night.

CHARITY   Good night, Oscar.
     (OSCAR *takes* CHARITY's *hand, then brings it up to his lips and kisses it*)

OSCAR   You're a lovely girl, Charity—*Sweet* Charity . . .
     (*He turns and runs off.* CHARITY *looks after him, then at her hand*)

CHARITY (*Obviously touched*)   Gee, for a weirdo—he's very nice. (*She turns and walks into the next set as it moves in*) Sweet Charity? Sweet Charity. Sweet Charity, that's what he calls me.

End of scene

CHARITY's *apartment*. SISSIE, NICKIE *and* HELENE *are lounging around filing their nails, doing their eyes and playing solitaire.* CHARITY's *dialogue starts as she moves into the set.*

CHARITY Can you imagine, I've gone out with the man now six times in the last two weeks and the most he ever tried was that hand-smooching business. Hey! that isn't a pass, is it?

(She starts to change clothes)

NICKIE Noo . . . Is it, Helene?

HELENE What?

NICKIE If a man kisses your hand. Would you classify that as a pass?

HELENE Well, that depends.

NICKIE On what?

HELENE On where your hand is when he kisses it.

NICKIE Hey! where was your hand?

CHARITY On the end of my arm. He has always behaved like a perfect gentleman.

HELENE What's a perfect gentleman?

CHARITY It's not my fault you've never met one.

NICKIE Hey! If he kisses your hand all the time, maybe he's after something.

CHARITY Like what?

NICKIE Your wristwatch.

CHARITY The only thing he's after is "Inner Contentment." And he wants me to help him find it.

NICKIE Honey, you sure picked up a couple of hundred-dollar words since you been going around with this goofball.

CHARITY Oscar is *not* a goofball! He is a highly complicated and very intelligent person.

NICKIE All right, so besides slobbering over your knuckles, what else can he do?

CHARITY He's in the Tax Accountancy profession. And he's also a graduate of C.C.N.Y.U. University . . .

NICKIE Ooh! Sounds like a goofball to me.

HELENE What does the goofball think of your vocation?

CHARITY My what?

HELENE Your chosen field of endeavor, child. Have you told him you're in the Rent-A-Body business?

CHARITY Oh, he thinks *nothing* of it.

HELENE and NICKIE She ain't told him.

CHARITY In the first place, he's too highly educated to be bothered with things like that. And in the second place, he knows because I already told him.

NICKIE (*Shocked*) That you're a dance hall hostess?

CHARITY Yes, yes!

NICKIE You told him?

CHARITY (*Very defensive*) Yes! Yes! I told him! I told him!

80

NICKIE When?

CHARITY *Next Sunday*. I'll tell him next Sunday—in Coney Island.

   (CHARITY *storms out. The girls look after her*)

HELENE She won't listen. That girl just will not listen.

NICKIE What do you think they talk about? When they're alone?

HELENE Talk? Honey, that girl's built for everything but conversation.

NICKIE Yeah. *He* probably does all the talking. Handing her those smooth lines like, "Baby, last night I dreamt you and I were in a cozy little cottage covered with clinging vines—"

HELENE And there we were—clinging more than the vines.

NICKIE And then he converts the convertible sofa and really goes to work.

BOTH Quote—

HELENE

   Baby, dream your dream;
   Close your eyes and try it.

NICKIE

   Dream of furniture;
   Dream that I can buy it.

HELENE

   That fancy bed you prayed for,
   Not only bought but paid for.

NICKIE

   Dream we sign the lease,
   Leave a small deposit.

81

HELENE

    Three and one-half rooms
    With a walk-in closet.

BOTH

    We'll ask the local Jet Set
    To dine on our dinette set.
    Right across the street

NICKIE

    There's a friendly bank; you
    Make a friendly loan

HELENE

    And the bank says, "Thank you."

BOTH

    Every Saturday
    We'll spend all our money.

HELENE

    Join the P.T.A.

NICKIE

    They will love you, honey.

BOTH

    Life will be frozen peaches and cream;
    Baby, dream your dream.

NICKIE   Can't you see that little love nest in three years?

HELENE   Yeah. She's feeding the chicks and he's ready to fly the coop!

BOTH

    Three fat, hungry kids,
    All in pink condition.

HELENE

So! Who's in the red?

NICKIE

That nice obstetrician.

BOTH

Big Daddy's fav'rite pastime—
He's had it for the last time.
Soon Daddy don't come home;
He says he's going bowling,
But a bowling ball

NICKIE

Is not what Daddy's rolling.

BOTH

Every night they fight;
Once they both exploded,
Then they both got tight.

HELENE

Tight? Hell, they got loaded!

BOTH

Well, who knows what will sour the cream
When you dream—your—
    (*Both laugh*)
But come to think of it,
How happy I would be
If someday I could find
The kind of guy who'd say to me
"Baby, dream your dream;
Close your eyes and try it."

HELENE

"Dream of three fat kids."

NICKIE

Brother, would I buy it!

BOTH

Life could be frozen peaches and cream
If only I could dream,
Dream, dream, dream a dream!

End of scene

A sign appears: "CONEY ISLAND." A number of people with balloons, kewpie dolls and ice cream cones pass by. One couple suddenly stops and looks up.

YOUNG MAN Hey, look at that!
(*Ad libs. A few other couples stop and look up. A* POLICEMAN *starts to push them back*)

POLICEMAN All right, move back; move back. Let the emergency car through, heh?

GIRL What's wrong, officer?

POLICEMAN Can't you see? (*He points up*) There's a fellow and a girl stuck up there on the Parachute Jump!
(*Ad libs. The lights black out on the group at the same time they come up on* CHARITY *and* OSCAR, *who are the couple stuck up on the Parachute Jump. They dangle from the sky strapped in a tiny two-seat contraption with a metal bar to hold onto. Perhaps the parachute above them can be seen.* OSCAR, *as usual, is in a panic*)

CHARITY Don't panic, Oscar. It's not gonna do you any good to panic. You won't panic, will you?

OSCAR No, I think there's a very good possibility I won't panic.

CHARITY You see, it's not like the elevator, Oscar. You've got plenty of air to breathe. Look at all the air you've got.
(*She looks around*)

OSCAR You're right—we've got enough air to last us for hours.

85

CHARITY   You're all right?

OSCAR   I'm fine—fine.

CHARITY   Good.

OSCAR   Charity. You're shaking.

CHARITY   All over.

OSCAR   Are you worried about me?

CHARITY   No. About me. I can't stand—

OSCAR   Heights?

CHARITY   Oh! Don't even say it!

OSCAR   It's all right, Charity. I'm right here with you.

CHARITY   You won't leave me, will you? I stayed with you in the elevator. Fair is fair.

OSCAR   I won't leave. I'll stay as long as you need me.

CHARITY   Gee, I've never been this scared before. I'm usually very calm in these situations.

OSCAR   And I'm usually very scared.

CHARITY   Now *I'm* the one who's scared.

OSCAR   And I'm unusually calm.

CHARITY   Maybe that's why I'm scared.

OSCAR   Because I'm calm?

CHARITY   (*Nods*)   When you know you have someone you can depend on, someone you know who can take care of you, you can afford to be scared. Oh, I've never had a someone like that before.

OSCAR   I've never had anyone who depended on me before.

CHARITY   Oh, boy! I'm depending on you now, Oscar.

86

OSCAR (*Manly*) Then sit back, relax and be scared. 'Cause I'm very dependable. (*Yells down*) Don't worry about the girl. *I'm* up here.

CHARITY Oh, Oscar, you're such a comfort.

OSCAR I do what I can.

CHARITY Hold on to me.

OSCAR For as long as you like.

CHARITY I'd like it for as long as we're up here.

OSCAR Then I hope we never come down.

CHARITY I really don't know what happened to me.

OSCAR That's funny because I know exactly what's happened to me. (*He sings*)
Here was a man
With no dream and no plan;
Then one crazy night I found
 Sweet Charity!

You make life fun for me;
Oh, what it's done for me,
Having you around,
 Sweet Charity!

Warm words I've never said
Lately pop off the top of my head—
 Incredible!

If, by and by,
You and I should be *we*
I could touch the sky—quite easily.
 So, if you are free,
 Sweet Charity,
Please belong to me.

87

> Sweet, Sweet Charity,
> Please belong to me!

CHARITY Oscar—maybe the reason I'm really scared is because I've got to tell you something about me that you may not like.

OSCAR There couldn't be anything about you I didn't like.
> (*He touches her hair*)

CHARITY You see, I'm not exactly with the Williamsburg Branch of the First National City Bank—

OSCAR You know, ever since I met you I knew there was something different about you. You have a quality in you, Charity, that I've never found in a girl before.

CHARITY In fact, I am definitely *not* with the Williamsburg Branch of the First National City Bank.

OSCAR Do you know what that quality is, Charity? It's purity. It's innocence. In you I have found pure innocence.

CHARITY As a matter of fact, I never, *never* been with the First National Williams of the Burg Bank.

OSCAR It's the truth, Charity. You're the last of a dying species. A virgin! Yes, a virgin in the most poetical sense of the word.
> (*They kiss*)

CHARITY . . . although we *do* have thirty-seven branches throughout the city.
> (*They kiss again*)

OSCAR and CHARITY
> Here was a man
> With no dream and no plan;

Then one crazy night I found
    Sweet Charity!

You make life fun for me;
Oh, what it's done for me,
Having you around,
    Sweet Charity!

Warm words I've never said
Lately pop off the top of my head—
    Incredible!

If, by and by,
You and I should be *we,*
I could touch the sky—quite easily!
    So, if you are free,
    Sweet Charity,
Please belong to me.
    Sweet, Sweet Charity,
Please belong to me!

BYSTANDERS
    Keep cool, you two up there.
    Know what I'd do up there,
    If I had you up there?
    They're quite a sight up there;
    They'll spend the night up there.
    They'll be all right up there.
    You wanna bet?
    He'll hold on to her!
    He'll hold on to her!

Blackout

The Fan-Dango Ballroom. HELENE *and the other host-esses are scattered about the lounge section. They are reading magazines, and they are all bored. There's not one customer in the place.*

HELENE Oh, boy! Ya can't make a dime in this joint.

HERMAN Psst. Psst. A live one.
　　　　(*Suddenly a lone young man enters. They all spring up and start to sing*)

GIRLS (*Sing*)
　　Do you wanna have
　　　　Fun, fun, fun?
　　How's about a few
　　　　Laughs, laughs . . .
　　　　(*The boy selects a girl and retires into a booth*)

HELENE Some business, heh? One fifteen-year-old dropout!
　　　　(NICKIE *enters with* ROSIE, *a new girl. This is her first night as a hostess. She's attractive and very nervous*)

NICKIE Girls! Girls! Good news. Besides stinkin' business, we now have a new, young, good-lookin' chick which we need like Idaho needs potatoes.

ROSIE (*Cheerfully to all*) Hello. I'm Rosie.

HELENE Not for long you ain't.
　　　　(*The others all say, "Hi."*)

ROSIE (*Looks around*) So this is the Ballroom.

NICKIE The Ballroom? That's right. This is where you'll

meet Prince Charming who'll carry you off on his white horse to Scarsdale. You should live so long.

ROSIE   It's awfully dark in here, isn't it?

HELENE   That's called "merchandising." When the goods are a little shopworn, don't put 'em in the window.

NICKIE   *You* got no problems, honey. You're *worth* six-fifty a half hour.

ROSIE   Is that what the men pay to dance with us?

HELENE   Uh-huh. Which you split with the owner, a nice, kindly Argentinian gentleman named Adolf Hitler.

NICKIE   Every penny of which you will earn. You dance a little, talk a little, roll your eyes a little, swivel your hips a little—and like this, you kill a lifetime.

ROSIE   Oh, I only expect to stay a few weeks.

NICKIE   (*Sarcastic*)   Oh, sure.

ROSIE   My boy friend's in California. When I save up enough money here, we're gonna get married.

HELENE   You'll make a sweet *old* couple.
      (CHARITY *enters, excitedly*)

CHARITY   Gather around, ladies—gather around and take a good look. It has happened to me. What every girl in this Ballroom dreams about, and it's happened to me.

HELENE   You've been drafted.

CHARITY   I'm in love. That's what's happened to me. I'm in love, I'm in love. I'm in love.

NICKIE   That's the eleven o'clock news. We listen to it every night.

CHARITY   Well, that was the last broadcast. This time it's different. This one is really serious.

CARMEN   Has he—talked about marriage?

CHARITY   Er—a—well, not in so many words.

ELAINE   How many?

CHARITY   None.

NICKIE   And now we turn to the local weather and sports.

HELENE   Look, kid, ya got any questions about this place— (*Pats* CHARITY) you just ask the housemother. She was with the original owners in 1794.

ROSIE   There's just one thing. I'm not a very good dancer.

NICKIE   Who dances? We defend ourselves to music.

CARMEN   All you gotta know is when they touch you, make like you're excited.

NICKIE   Of course a cute-lookin' thing like you can always go into the "extra-curricular" business.

CHARITY   What are you telling her a thing like *that* for? (*To* ROSIE) Hey, kid. You want some good advice, get out of this crummy joint—before you wind up like the rest of us.

HELENE   Don't look at me; I was *always* like this.
         (*A man enters the Ballroom alone.* HERMAN *signals from his booth*)

HERMAN   Hey! C'mon.

FRENCHY   A live one!
         (*They all get up*)

ROSIE   What do I do?

NICKIE   Sugar, from here on it's every man for himself. (*All the girls move down to the rail.* ROSIE *and* CHARITY *are standing side by side*)

HELENE (*To the man*)   Hey, can I talk to you for a minute?

SUZANNE   Got a cigarette? Come here. I wanna tell you something.

FRENCHY   Ooh, so tall. Americans always so tall.

NICKIE   Chicago, right? I can always tell a home-town boy.

CARMEN (*Snapping her fingers*)   You look like a good dancer.
(*The man walks silently up and down the line-up of girls. He goes back and seems to be making up his mind between* CHARITY *and* ROSIE. *The man finally chooses* ROSIE, *gets his ticket and goes off to a booth with her*)

NICKIE   Sure learns fast, for a kid.

CHARITY   She doesn't look like such a kid to me.

HELENE   Ooh, touchy-touchy!

CARMEN   Sore just 'cause you came in second?

CHARITY   I'm sore 'cause I came in at all. Boy, am I sick of this musical snake pit.

NICKIE (*Bryn Mawr-ish*)   Well. You can always go back to Mummy and Daddy's place in Southampton.

CHARITY   I'll be getting out a lot sooner than any of you think.
(*Two men walk in*)

HERMAN   Hey!

ELAINE   Psst. Psst. *Ole*, girls. Two more bulls in the ring. (*The other girls move down to the rail again.* NICKIE *goes to* CHARITY *and puts her arm around her shoulder*)

NICKIE   (*To* CHARITY)   Look busy, Baby. Der Führer is watching.
   (*She means* HERMAN)

CHARITY   Let him watch. Let him fire me. You think I care?

NICKIE   Yeah, I think you care.

CHARITY   Well, I don't. I don't care. (*Angrily*) I cared for eight years but I do not care any more. And I'll tell you why I don't care any more. Because I don't like it here. I like you and I like Helene and I like the girls and I even like Herman. But *I don't like it here*. This-is-not-a-nice-place! And I do not intend to spend another day of my life in a place that is not a nice place!

NICKIE   What are you trying to say?

CHARITY   I am trying to say that I have made up what's left of my mind. I've made my decision. I know exactly what I have to do.

HELENE   What exactly do you have to do?

CHARITY   I have to get out. Understand? *Out!* Now! Tonight. This minute.

NICKIE   You mean you're goin'—

CHARITY   I mean, "You're damned right I'm goin'." (*She goes.* NICKIE *shrugs and moves down to the rail as the lights dim and a single light hits* CHARITY. *She moves downstage and the Ballroom moves off behind her*) The only trouble is, I don't know where. (*She sings*)

94

Where am I going?
And what will I find?
What's in this grab bag
That I call my mind?
What am I doing alone on the shelf?
Ain't it a shame, but
No one's to blame but myself!
Which way is clear?
When you've lost your way
Year after year . . .
Do I keep falling in love
For just the kick of it,
Staggering through the thin and thick of it,
Hating each old and tired trick of it?
Know what I am? I'm good and sick of it!
Where am I going?
Why do I care?
Run to the Bronx
Or Washington Square.
No matter where I run,
I meet myself there.
Looking inside me
What do I see?
Anger and hope and doubt.
What am I all about
    And
Where am I going?
You tell me!

End of scene

95

CHARITY *is in Times Square. At the end of the first chorus of her song, a phone booth moves on. She puts in a coin and dials quickly.*

CHARITY (*Into the phone, frantically*) Hello? Western Union? I want to send a collect telegram. To Mr. Oscar Lindquist. 411 East Seventy-fourth Street. New York City. The message is: "Dear Oscar, I must talk to you right away but since I know you don't have a telephone, I am sending you this collect wire . . . I've got to know where I stand. What are your intentions? Are you just playing around with me? Because if you are, what the hell was with all that handkissing?" Handkissing! Yeah! I think it's one word . . . "Please, please meet me at one A.M. in Barney's Chile Hacienda so we can discuss a matter of utmost urgency . . ." Sign it: "Charity." No, make that "*Sweet* Charity." (*She hangs up and speaks to herself*) He's got to come. *He's got to!* He won't!

(*She finishes the song*)
Looking inside me,
What do I see?
Anger and hope and doubt.
What am I all about
    And
Where am I going?
You tell me!

End of scene

*A sign appears: "THE PROPOSAL." It disappears.
When the lights come up, we are in Barney's Chile Hacienda, a small Mexican restaurant on Eighth Avenue. There
are two booths against the wall.* OSCAR *sits alone in a booth,
nervously glancing at his watch.* CHARITY *enters. She looks
at* OSCAR. *He sees her and gets up.*

OSCAR   Charity, I—
(*But* CHARITY *walks right past him and sits in the
booth behind him so that they are directly back to
back*)

CHARITY (*Doesn't look at him*)   Sit down, Oscar.

OSCAR (*Surprised*)   Aren't you going to sit with me?

CHARITY (*Tense*)   I have some very important things to
say to you, Oscar, and if I have to look in your eyes I
don't think I'll be able to say them.
(OSCAR *wants to protest, but he sits down back to
back with her.* BARNEY *returns with a cup of coffee
and looks quizzically at the way they are sitting*)

BARNEY   You alone, Miss?

OSCAR (*Without turning*)   She's with me.
(BARNEY *looks at them both, puzzled at first; then
he shrugs and exits*)

CHARITY   Oscar, I had to see you to tell you—I can't see
you any more.

OSCAR (*Starts to turn*)   What?

CHARITY   Don't look at me. Don't look at me. (*He turns*

97

back to back again) Aren't you going to ask me why? Aren't you going to ask me why I can't see you any more?

OSCAR   Why can't you see me any more?

CHARITY   Never mind. I'll tell you. Because we're not getting anywhere, that's why. And we're not *going* to get anywhere either, because you don't even know where I've been. Oscar, I don't, never have and probably never will *work in a bank.*

OSCAR   Oh?

CHARITY   I don't even have a bank *account.* I keep my money in an empty can of Chase and Sanborn coffee.

OSCAR   Charity—

CHARITY   And do you have any idea of how I earn that money? Do you? Heh?

OSCAR   You're a dance hall hostess.

CHARITY   I'm a dance hall hostess. I work in a dance hall. I dance with strange men and talk to them and drink with them and (*She suddenly realizes what he said*) That's right! How did you know?

OSCAR   I've known it for a week now. I was riding a bus one night, saw you, jumped off, and before I could catch you I saw you go into this dance hall. I went in and stood in the corner. You were sitting in a booth with some man. You were laughing and giggling. I didn't stay very long—an hour or so. That night when I went home, I tried very very hard to hate you, Charity—but I couldn't do it. I just couldn't hate you.

CHARITY   Maybe you'll have better luck tonight. Do you know what *other* business some of the girls are in?

OSCAR I'm not interested.

CHARITY Don't you want to ask me if I am too?

OSCAR It's not important.

CHARITY (*Indignant*) Not important? Well, it is to *me*. I'm in love with you, Oscar, and I'm not going to waste being in love with some jerk who isn't interested enough to find out if I really am what I'm hinting I *might* be. Don't look at me.

OSCAR Charity, I don't care what you are or what you did. All I know is I want to marry you.

CHARITY Let's settle one thing at a time, heh? I am *not* in any other business. All I sell is my *time*. But just to keep the record straight, I am not a poetical virgin!
(*She suddenly bursts into tears*)

OSCAR Charity, Charity, please don't cry. I believe you.

CHARITY (*Crying*) I know you believe me. I'm crying about that other part.

OSCAR What other part?

CHARITY That *marrying* part! I didn't hear it the first time.

OSCAR Marry me!

CHARITY (*Still crying*) Oh, Oscar, you're not making fun of me, are you? Because asking a girl to marry her is one of her most sensitive areas. And you shouldn't say it unless you really mean it. Because you can seriously hurt people kidding around like that. And I'll tell you the truth, Oscar. I don't really think I can stand another injury of that nature.

OSCAR Charity, for the first time I'm happy "inside." *Really* happy—and it's all because of you.

CHARITY (*Turns*) Oh, Oscar—

OSCAR Don't look at me! I can get pretty emotional too, you know! Give me your hand. (*She puts her hand down. He gropes backwards, feels it and clasps it into his*) You know what we're gonna do, Charity? We're gonna get out of this city.

CHARITY Oh, I'd like that.

OSCAR Get a little place in the country.

CHARITY I'd like that.

OSCAR We don't need much money. I could get a little gas station. I've always loved cars . . .

CHARITY You'd like that.

OSCAR Maybe get a Mobilgas franchise—with the big red and white sign.

CHARITY I'd like that . . .

OSCAR What really counts is that we'll be together.

CHARITY That's what really counts.

OSCAR Forget your past. Forget what you did before.

CHARITY I forgot it. It's forgotten.

OSCAR Some men could never do that, Charity. But not me.

CHARITY Not you.

OSCAR I promise I'll never mention it again as long as I live.

CHARITY I'd like that.

OSCAR   Because I need you, Charity—I need you and I love you. (*The lights begin to fade on everything but* CHARITY) There's this little place on Route 66 in Passaic . . .

> (*He fades out.* CHARITY *walks out of the scene and comes downstage. The music helps build the moment*)

CHARITY   He loves me! (*She moves to one side*) Someone loves me! (*She runs to the other side. She's shouting it to the whole world now*) Someone loves me! (*All her joy and emotion seem to pour out of her. She sings*)

Somebody loves me!
My heart is beating so fast;
All kinds of music is pouring out of me.
Somebody loves me at last!

I'm a brass band
I'm a harpsichord
I'm a clarinet
I'm the Philadelphia Orchestra
I'm the Modern Jazz Quartet
I'm the band from
Macy's big parade
A big Count Basie blast
I'm the bells of St. Peter's in Rome
I'm tissue paper on a comb.
And all kinds of music keeps pouring out of me 'cause
Somebody loves me at last!
    (*She dances, then sings again*)
Somebody loves me at last!
    (*She dances again*)
Somebody loves me—at last!

End of scene

The Fan-Dango Ballroom. Everyone is scurrying around.

ALICE Shhhh, she's coming. She's coming!
(*Everyone ad libs*)

HERMAN Shhh. Okay, everybody, hide and be quiet. I want this to be a God-damned surprise party. (*Tells everyone where to go*) And keep your heads down!

MAN Hey, Herman, what about you?

HERMAN Oh, yeah; I forgot.
(*He ducks behind a banquette.* CHARITY *walks in carrying her suitcase. She looks around*)

CHARITY Hey. Hello? Hello, I'm going. Anyone here to say goodbye to me? No? (*There is no answer. She shrugs*) Okay. Well, goodbye!
(*She turns to go when suddenly twenty-five people spring out of nowhere and shout, "Surprise!"* CHARITY *screams in fright. All the hostesses are there and about ten men including* HERMAN, *a* COP, *a couple of* WAITERS, *a few* DELIVERY MEN, *a* DOORMAN *and a couple of regular customers*)

HERMAN You didn't think we'd let you go without givin' ya a little party, did ya?

CHARITY A party? For me? Oh, you shouldn't have. You shouldn't have.

NICKIE (*To* HELENE) I told you we shouldn't have.
(*There is a fanfare as two men pick* CHARITY *up. Someone else brings out a high stool and they set* CHARITY *down on it in the center of the room. She*

yells out, "Hey, what're you doing? Put me down."
They place a box down for HERMAN, *who stands*
on it)

HERMAN   And now, through the courtesy of the hostesses
of the Fan-Dango Ballroom, Local 107, the waiters, the
janitor, Joe the bouncer, Harry the Cop, and our three
regular customers since 1954—we present (*Another fan-*
fare) . . . a seventeen-dollar cake.
    (*A huge cake is wheeled out on a cart, as everyone*
oohs and ahs. They place it in front of CHARITY)

CHARITY (*Excited*)   Beautiful! (*She bends over and reads*
the inscription) "Happy Birthday Angelo?"

NICKIE (*Whacks* HERMAN *across the shoulders*)   You
couldn't get a new cake, you cheapskate?
    (*There are ad libs*)

HERMAN   All right, all right. I didn't know she was
leavin' till this morning.
    (*They all shout, "Cheapskate!" at* HERMAN)

CHARITY   Never mind. It's the sentiment that counts. Herman, Angelo and I thank you very much.

HERMAN (*Smiles at her*)   For a broad, you gotta lotta class.

CARMEN (*To* NICKIE)   The present. Give her the present.
    (*There are more ad libs*)

NICKIE   Awright. Awright. (HERMAN *gets off the box and*
NICKIE *gets up on it*) Charity Hope Valentine, we who
have lived with you, undressed with you, suffered the
indignities of this crummy joint with you (*The girls all*
yell, "Yeah!") . . . who have come to know you, and to
love you—on this, your nuptial eve (*More ad libs*) . . .

Ah shaddup. We just want to wish you—Oh, my God, I'm gonna cry.
(*She cries*)

HELENE Will ya quit slobberin' all over the cake.

NICKIE (*Crying*) I can't help it. I'm gonna miss her.

HELENE We all are. (HELENE *pulls her off the box*) Get down and I'll give the speech. (HELENE *gets on the box. There are ad libs*) Charity, honey (*She starts crying*) . . . Oh God, we're gonna miss you, kid.
(CARMEN *pulls her down and gets up*)

CARMEN So we bought you this little present. Which I picked out.
(*She hands* CHARITY *a box*)

CHARITY For me? A wedding gift?
(*They all yell, "Open it."* CHARITY *opens the box and, to her surprise, takes out a little baby's size-one snowsuit.* CHARITY *looks puzzled*)

NICKIE (*Angrily, to* CARMEN) What the hell kind of wedding gift is that?

CARMEN (*Shrugs*) I thought she was pregnant. Isn't that why she's getting married?
(*They all hoot her down*)

CHARITY Oh, no! It's the best wedding present I ever got.
(*They all applaud and she cries*)

HERMAN (*Shouts for quiet*) It ain't often that one of our girls leaves to marry a nice, respectable guy. In fact, this is the first time it ever happened. And so, as a parting gesture, our three regular customers since 1954 would like a farewell dance with our own bride-to-be, Miss Charity Valentine. (*The three regular customers all*

take turns dancing with CHARITY. *In the midst of this,*
OSCAR *walks in and watches.* HERMAN *sees him and walks
over)* I'm sorry, Mac, this is a private party.

OSCAR   I know. I'm her—I'm here to take her away.

HERMAN   Yeah? Hey, Charity. Did you call for a cab?

CHARITY *(Sees him and rushes to him)* Oscar! It's him,
everybody. This is the fellow. He's the one. It's him.
(She puts her arm in his) He's it—him.

OSCAR *(Embarrassed)*   Hello.
    (The girls all circle him and ogle him)

NICKIE *(While still shaking* OSCAR'S *hand)*   He's taking
our baby away . . .
    (She cries)

CHARITY   Oscar, I want you to meet our boss Herman,
affectionately known as Der Führer!

OSCAR   Pleasure.

HERMAN   Likewise. How about a beer? Hey, somebody
get a beer for Mr.—er—Mr.—?

CHARITY   Lindquist.

HERMAN   That's right, Lindquist. Sit down.
    *(He seats them. After seating them he begins a
    speech)*

ALL *(With general ad libs)* Yeah. Hear, hear. Give a
speech. *(They sing)*
   It's tough for a loud-mouth mug like me,
   Who all the time bellows like a bull,
   To make with the words
   About the "Missus-to-be!"
   When what *you* think is an empty heart—is full!

Tomorrow when you say: "I do." . . . I'll die!
I'm almost too ashamed to tell you why!

I love to cry at weddings!
How I love to cry at weddings!
I walk into a chapel
And get happily hysterical.
The ushers and attendants,
The family dependents,
I see them and I start to sniff.
Have you an extra handkerchief?
And all through the service,
While the bride and groom look nervous,
Tears of joy are streaming down my face.

MIKE

Down his face.

HERMAN

I love to cry at weddings—
Anybody's wedding.

ALL

Any time! Any where! Any place!

ROSIE

I always weep at weddings!
I'm a soggy creep at weddings!
Ah! What's as sweet and sloppy as:
"Oh, Promise Me" . . . and all that jazz?

TWO GIRLS

The man you rest your head with,
The man you share your bed with
Is married to you—so you know
He won't jump up and dress and blow!

NICKIE

I could marry Herman—

HELENE

> And be permanently sorry!

NICKIE

> We would make a really lousy pair;
> But, gee, I want a wedding,
> Any kind of wedding—any time, any place, any
> where!

ALL

> And all through the service,
> While the bride and groom look nervous,
> Tears of joy are streaming down my face.
> I love to cry at weddings—
> Anybody's wedding.
> Any time! Any where! Any place!
>
> I love to cry at weddings!
> How I love to cry at weddings!
> I walk into a chapel
> And get happily hysterical.
> The ushers and attendants,
> The family dependents,
> I see them and I start to sniff.
> Please let me use your handkerchief!
> And all through the service,
> While the bride and groom are nervous,
> I drink champagne and sing "Sweet Adeline."
> I love to cry at weddings!
> Everybody's wedding!
> Just as long as it's not mine!

> > (CHARITY *goes around saying her goodbyes.* HELENE
> > *and* NICKIE *stand away.* CHARITY *comes up behind
> > them and slips* VIDAL's *picture into* HELENE's *hand
> > and the top hat into* NICKIE's)

ALL (*Sing softly*)
I love to cry at weddings—
Anybody's wedding.
Any time! Any where! Any place!
   (CHARITY *and* OSCAR *are gone*)
I love to cry at weddings!
How I love to cry at weddings!
I walk into a chapel
And get happily hysterical.
The ushers and attendants,
The family dependents,
I see them and I start to sniff.
Have you an extra handkerchief?
And all through the service,
While the bride and groom look nervous,
Tears of joy are streaming down my face.
I love to cry at weddings—
Anybody's wedding.
Any time! Any where! Any place!

End of scene

A sign appears. It reads: "PLANS." It disappears. Two lights pick up OSCAR *and* CHARITY, *hand in hand in the park. The rest of the stage is dark.* CHARITY *is glowing and speaks rapidly, filled with emotion. There is music playing underneath.*

CHARITY   Oh, Oscar. I didn't like the first half of my life much but the second half sure is getting good. (*Snaps her fingers, remembering something*) Oh, I knew I had something to show you (*Fishes through her purse and takes out a card*) —a joint bank account. I deposited the entire can of Chase and Sanborn. So that's my entire dowry. The point I'm trying to get across, Oscar Lindquist, is that I'm very happy.

OSCAR   (*Uncomfortably*) Charity, there is something I have to tell you.

CHARITY   Oh, I've been doing all the talking. Okay, it's your turn, Oscar.

OSCAR   Charity, I'm very fond of you; you know that. And I find you unique—

CHARITY   That's me!

OSCAR   —and different and sweet and wonderful and tender—and I just can't marry you. Did you hear me, Charity?

CHARITY   (*Quickly*) Yeah, I heard you. I heard you.

OSCAR   I can't, Charity—I can't go through with it.

CHARITY   All right, Oscar, I know this isn't a joke because you certainly wouldn't joke about a thing like that at a time like this. It couldn't be a joke because it would be a very rotten joke. But I can't figure what else it could be. Oscar, is it a joke?

OSCAR   This is not easy for me, Charity. Not easy at all.

CHARITY   I know it's not easy, Oscar—but is it a joke?

OSCAR (*Irritated*)   It is *not* a joke. It is *no* joke!

CHARITY (*Mumbles*)   It's no joke.

OSCAR   I thought this time it would be different. But it's not. It's the same. It's always the same.

CHARITY   What's the same?

OSCAR   The other men. I always get this far and then I start thinking about the other men . . .

CHARITY   What other men?

OSCAR (*Gently*)   You know what other men!

CHARITY (*Pauses*)   But Oscar, you said . . .

OSCAR   Oh, I know I kept saying it didn't matter, because I thought if I said it enough I could convince myself it was true.

CHARITY   That certainly makes sense to me, Oscar.

OSCAR   It's not your fault, Charity. You're a wonderful girl.

CHARITY (*Hopefully*)   I am?

OSCAR   But it's *my* problem, Charity. I have this neurosis —a mental block.

CHARITY   There's a lot of that going around.

OSCAR (*With self-anger*)   But I have this childish, incomprehensible, idiotic, fixation about purity. In this day and age? It's laughable, isn't it? (*She laughs*) It's not funny. But every time I think of you—with all those other men—

CHARITY   Oscar, you're making a mountain out of a couple of guys.

OSCAR   How many?

CHARITY   What?

OSCAR (*Shouts*)   How many? I want to know *exactly* how many.

CHARITY   Gee, when you yell like that, I can't think. (*She starts to count on her fingers*) Frank, Harry, Sidney . . . How far back do you want me to go?

OSCAR (*Covers his eyes in agony*)   Oh, my God, don't tell me. I don't want to hear.

CHARITY   Oscar, I know I'm not very bright. I could go to night school. We could be so happy in that gas station; I know it. On the days you felt "sick," you could stay in bed and I'd work the pumps. I've got so much to give. Let me give it to you.
(*She falls to her knees, pleading*)

OSCAR   Charity, get up. You're too good to be on your knees to me.

CHARITY (*With a weak smile*)   Give the little girl a break, heh?

OSCAR   Together, I'd destroy you. Sooner or later it would start again, and I'd hound you day and night. "What were their names?" "How long did you know them before?" "How did you feel when they—"

CHARITY   You could ask me *anything*. I won't hide a thing. I'll tell you everything you want to know.

OSCAR You'd like that, wouldn't you? I'd get all the pretty details, wouldn't I? Give you quite a thrill, heh?

CHARITY You won't get one word out of me, not a word. Don't you see, Oscar, I'm very flexible. I can go either way.

OSCAR There's only one way to go with me. To destruction. Marry me and I'll destroy you, Charity.

CHARITY That's okay. I'm not doing much now, anyway.

OSCAR But the one shred of decency left in me won't let me destroy you. I must save you from me. I'm doing this for your own good, Charity. Run. Run. *I'm saving you, Charity—saving you!* (*He has forced her down to the apron. He pushes her into the orchestra pit. A sign appears: "DITTO."* OSCAR *leans over and looks down*) Woops. (*He starts running in all different directions, then goes back to the pit. He starts to run again, then goes back to the pit*) Charity, I feel sick about this. You may not believe that, but I feel just terrible. (*He backs away from the pit*) A wonderful girl—so understanding. They don't make them like that any more.

> (*He goes off. The stage is empty for a moment. One of* CHARITY's *hands emerges from the pit. Then the other. Finally she lifts herself on the edge of the stage, her legs dangling into the pit. She is wringing wet*)

CHARITY Did you ever have one of those days? (*She wrings some water out of her hair and her clothing. She sighs again*) At least I didn't get tattooed again. (*She picks herself up and starts to pull herself together, then she notices she still has her purse. She opens it up, looks inside and smiles*) . . . And I still have my dowry. (*Optimistically*) . . . Maybe things are beginning to pick up for me. (*Suddenly we see a shimmering light and hear an eerie musical effect—and lo and behold, before our very eyes at stage left appears, believe it or not—the* GOOD FAIRY—*wearing a flowing gold cape and silver slippers and carrying a wand.* CHARITY *can scarcely believe her eyes. She rubs them and looks again. The* GOOD FAIRY *is still there*) Hey! Hey, you're really not—?

GOOD FAIRY (*She waves the wand at* CHARITY) Tonight! Tonight! It will *all* happen tonight!

CHARITY (*Believing, like a little girl*) What? What'll happen tonight?

GOOD FAIRY Dreams will come true tonight! Tonight! Tonight!
(*She waves the wand at* CHARITY *again and throws a handful of stardust at her. The* GOOD FAIRY *then turns and goes. On her back is a large sign that reads, "Watch 'The Good Fairy' tonight—8 o'clock —CBS." She flutters off the stage.* CHARITY *turns, smiles and shrugs as the music of "Charity's Theme" starts. The general lighting fades, leaving one light on* CHARITY. *She picks up her suitcase and begins to dance as she did in the beginning of the first act.*

As she dances, a sign appears in the same style as the first signs that appeared in the show. It reads:
"AND SO SHE LIVED
. . . HOPEFULLY
. . . EVER AFTER."
She strikes a pose in silhouette as in the opening scene)

Curtain

1. Redox
2. Spectator - no change in Oxidation state
3. Hydrogen (H_2)
4. Oxygen (O_2) (Balance equation)